I0448735

S. Hrg. 113–76

PUERTO RICO

HEARING

BEFORE THE

COMMITTEE ON
ENERGY AND NATURAL RESOURCES
UNITED STATES SENATE

ONE HUNDRED THIRTEENTH CONGRESS

FIRST SESSION

TO

RECEIVE TESTIMONY ON THE NOVEMBER 6, 2012, REFERENDUM ON THE POLITICAL STATUS OF PUERTO RICO AND THE ADMINISTRATION'S RESPONSE

AUGUST 1, 2013

Printed for the use of the
Committee on Energy and Natural Resources

U.S. GOVERNMENT PRINTING OFFICE

82–719 PDF   WASHINGTON : 2013

For sale by the Superintendent of Documents, U.S. Government Printing Office
Internet: bookstore.gpo.gov   Phone: toll free (866) 512–1800; DC area (202) 512–1800
Fax: (202) 512–2104   Mail: Stop IDCC, Washington, DC 20402–0001

CONTENTS

STATEMENTS

PUERTO RICO

THURSDAY, AUGUST 1, 2013

U.S. SENATE,
COMMITTEE ON ENERGY AND NATURAL RESOURCES,
Washington, DC.

The committee met, pursuant to notice, at 9:51 a.m. in room SD–366, Dirksen Senate Office Building, Hon. Ron Wyden, chairman, presiding.

OPENING STATEMENT OF HON. RON WYDEN, U.S. SENATOR FROM OREGON

The CHAIRMAN. The committee will come to order.

Senator Murkowski and I want to welcome our witnesses. This morning the committee is going to hear testimony on the results of last November's vote on Puerto Rico's political status and on the President's response.

Puerto Rico has been an "unincorporated territory" of the United States since the conclusion of the Spanish American War, 115 years ago. After 115 years it is clearly time for Puerto Rico to determine what political path it will take. The question of whether Puerto Rico should become a State or a sovereign Nation and whether there are other options defines much of the political debate today on the islands.

Puerto Rico faces huge economic and social challenges. Per capita income is stuck at about half that of the poorest U.S. State. The violent crime rate is well above the national average and rising. The lack of resolution of Puerto Rico's status, not only distracts from addressing these and other issues, it contributes to them.

As the most recent reports from the President's Task Force on Puerto Rico's status found and I quote, identifying the most effective means of assisting the Puerto Rican economy depends on resolving the ultimate question of status."

95 years after receiving U.S. citizenship, Puerto Ricans have achieved leadership in the U.S. military, in business, in the Congress, on the Supreme Court and in many other prestigious positions. But for Puerto Rico to meet its economic and social challenges and to achieve its full potential, this debate over status needs to be settled.

Puerto Rico must either exercise full self-government as a sovereign Nation or achieve equality among the states of the Union.

The current relationship undermines our country's moral standing in the world. For a Nation founded on the principles of democracy and the consent of the governed, how much longer can America allow a condition to persist in which nearly 4 million U.S. citi-

(1)

zens do not have a vote in the government that makes the national laws which effect their daily lives? That is the question.

Today the committee will hear testimony about the most recent effort to resolve the status question, last November's vote.

I expect to hear two vastly different views about what the results of the vote mean. However, there is no disputing that a majority of the voters in Puerto Rico, 54 percent, have clearly expressed their opposition to continuing the current territorial status. Given that fact, I agree with the President's proposal to resolve this dispute through a federally sponsored referendum.

I also agree that the ballot questions should be reviewed by the Department of Justice to ensure that the options are not inconsistent with the Constitution, laws, and policies of our country.

The Justice Department review is essential to ensuring the proposed new commonwealth status or a proposal with similar features will not be on the ballot.

The new commonwealth option continues to be advocated as a viable option by some. It is not. Persistence in supporting this option—after it has been rejected is inconsistent with the U.S. Constitution by the U.S. Justice Department, by the bipartisan leadership of this committee, by the House and by the Clinton, Bush, and Obama Administrations—undermines resolution of Puerto Rico's status question.

The rejection of the current territory status last November leaves Puerto Rico with only two options: Statehood under U.S. sovereignty or some form of separate national sovereignty.

The federally sponsored vote should be simple and straight-forward and reflect these two choices.

Today we will hear from the Presidents of Puerto Rico's 3 principle political parties.

Governor Padilla of the Commonwealth Party.

Resident Commissioner Pierluisi, of the Statehood Party.

Former Senator Berrios of the Independence Party.

The full written statement of all our witnesses will be entered into the record. I'm going to ask each of you to summarize your oral remarks to not more than 5 minutes.

But let us first have the opportunity for Senator Murkowski to make her opening remarks.

[The prepared statement of Senator Manchin follows:]

PREPARED STATEMENT OF HON. JOE MANCHIN, III, U.S. SENATOR FROM WEST VIRGINIA

Thank you Chairman Wyden and Ranking Member Murkowski for holding this hearing today on the political status of Puerto Rico.

As a former governor, I am uniquely aware of the great responsibility of that office. The voters, through their constitutionally granted right to free and fair elections, choose a governor to carry out the duties of the office and to handle the needs of the state. The governor is accountable and responsible to the people of the state. And if those people, the voters, are not happy with the governor, the election process grants them the ability to change course.

The issue of Puerto Rican political status is undoubtedly important. However, I would bet that most Puerto Ricans would rank job creation, education, and strengthening the economy as the most pressing needs on their mind. I trust the Governor is dedicated to addressing both those needs and the question of political status.

On this issue of status, any referendum effort should adhere strictly to our democratic principles of impartiality and inclusiveness. It seems to me the most recent referendum does not meet these benchmarks. I understand Governor Garcia Padilla supports a referendum process that is fair and open, as would I. If another referendum is called in the Commonwealth, the people of Puerto Rico should be presented with clear and unambiguous options for such a significant decision, so as to match our shared democratic principles.

I hope that all of our witnesses here today will continue to work with this committee so that we can ensure a fair and open discussion on the issue of Puerto Rico's political status.

STATEMENT OF HON. LISA MURKOWSKI, U.S. SENATOR FROM ALASKA

Senator MURKOWSKI. Thank you, Mr. Chairman.

Good morning and to our distinguished panelists, welcome to the committee.

Mr. Chairman, as you noted this hearing is a direct result of the November 2012 plebiscite that was held in Puerto Rico on their political status. It's an issue that I have taken an interest in and perhaps feel a sense of kinship as I believe I'm the only sitting United States Senator, who was actually born in a territory. So that dates me a little bit, but I'm OK with birthdays. It's better than the alternative.

It's long been my position that the process for determining Puerto Rico's preferred political status should come from Puerto Rico and not from Washington, DC, just as the residents of Alaska and Hawaii did as the last two states that were admitted to the Union.

Now that the plebiscite has been held it's clear to me that a majority of Puerto Ricans do not favor the current territorial status as evidenced by the first question on the ballot. The result of the second question, however, is not as clear to me nor is it certain that any of the valid status options would receive a majority vote.

When I use the term valid status options, I'm referring to the continuation of the current Commonwealth status, statehood, independence and free association similar to what the United States has with the Marshall Islands, Micronesia and Palau.

Back in 2010 I joined with our former Chairman, Senator Bingaman in outlining these options to the President as the only 4 status options available for Puerto Rico's future relations with the United States. It was my preference leading up to the November 2012 plebiscite that the ballot have one question with each of the 4 options listed. Puerto Rican government, however, chose to go with the two question ballot. As a supporter of the process being driven by Puerto Rico, I respect that decision.

But what we learned is that the current status does not have majority support. Beyond that I don't believe that we can draw any definitive conclusions about the plebiscite results.

The President's FY'14 budget request included 2.5 million for another plebiscite in Puerto Rico. But even if a new plebiscite is held, it is the Puerto Rican legislature that will determine how that ballot will appear. If that path is chosen I would encourage a format that is fair to all valid options.

I look forward to hearing from the representatives that we have here this morning again, a very distinguished panel on a very important issue to the people of Puerto Rico.

The CHAIRMAN. Thank you very much, Senator Murkowski.

Let us begin with the Governor, Governor Padilla.

Then let's hear from the Resident Commissioner, Pierluisi.

Senator Berrios will then proceed.

So, Governor, welcome.

We'll make your prepared remarks a part of the hearing record in their entirety. Please proceed, if you would for maybe 5 minutes or so. I think you'll get questions from Senators.

STATEMENT OF HON. ALEJANDRO GARCÍA-PADILLA, GOVERNOR OF THE COMMONWEALTH OF PUERTO RICO AND PRESIDENT OF THE POPULAR DEMOCRATIC PARTY

Mr. PADILLA. Thank you, Mr. Chairman, Ranking Member Murkowski and members of the committee. The stated purpose of this hearing is to receive testimony on the status referendum that took place in Puerto Rico this past November and the Administration's response.

As Governor I will prefer to testify on measures to create jobs or fighting crime or energy which is so important for Puerto Rico and the agenda of this committee. The people of Puerto Rico feel the same way.

However, I welcome this opportunity to set the record straight.

The 2012 status referendum was crafted by the Statehood Party, then in power in Puerto Rico to force an artificial majority for statehood. The process they chose excluding the Commonwealth from the ballot is the same suggestion by the delegate Pierluisi 4 years ago, Commonwealth was wanted there.

That process was swiftly rejected in the House and the Senate because it's disenfranchised, disenfranchised a majority of the voters.

When the bill came to the Senate, Delegate Pierluisi told this very same committee regarding the second vote and I quote. "Let's make sure that nobody is left out, nobody who wants to support a valid option. The current statute call it the Commonwealth is one option." End of quote.

His running mate, former Governor Fortuño, was more emphatic. I quote. "The current statue will stand equally alongside the other possible status alternatives." End of quote.

Those Democratic values stated in this room were not repeated in Puerto Rico. Out of Congress side they delegated to exclude the Commonwealth.

Nevertheless, you can see through the numbers. Almost 1.9 million voters participated, a little more than 800 thousand voted for statehood. Statehood rallied 44.4 percent.

Blank ballots 26.5.

What they call sovereign Commonwealth, 24.3 percent.

Independence 4 percent.

This is the take away. Statehood received only 44.4 percent of the ballots casted because of the way the plebiscite was asserted. Many of us ask in the populous to cast the ballots blank. Other leaders in my party asked that they vote for sovereign Commonwealth.

Combined ballots cast for sovereign Commonwealth and blank ballots were a majority of the votes.

The White House Task Force report has warned that removing the Commonwealth option from the ballot and I quote. "Would rise real questions about the vote legitimacy." End of quote.

Such warning proved to be correct.

To set the record straight the Puerto Rico legislature adopted a current resolution 24 which I'm pleased to submit with my statement.

History, Mr. Chairman, has taught that only consensus driven process would succeed in Washington. We welcome the Administration's request for a new vote. We look forward to working with the Department of Justice to ensure a process that is fair, transparent and Democratic.

I commend President Obama for proposing a new plebiscite with fairness to all status options. I also thank the White House for working closely with us on the keys that's affecting Puerto Rico, fighting crime, energy, health, education, jobs.

I respectfully urge this Senate to follow President Obama's recommendation. What Puerto Ricans want is a true self determination process, not political games. What happened in November was a political game.

This, Mr. Chairman, is the way to go. As Governor I defend the right of pro-statehooders, pro-independence option and pro-Commonwealthers to have their option on the ballot. That's the way to go.

[The prepared statement of Mr. García-Padilla follows:]

PREPARED STATEMENT OF HON. ALEJANDRO GARCÍA-PADILLA, GOVERNOR OF THE COMMONWEALTH OF PUERTO RICO AND PRESIDENT OF THE POPULAR DEMOCRATIC PARTY

Dear members of the Senate Committee on Energy and Natural Resources:

You have requested my opinion on the plebiscite celebrated in Puerto Rico on November 6, 2012 and President Obama's proposal for an appropriation of $2,500,000 for the celebration of a new plebiscite. I will address the aforementioned matter in that order.

I. THE 2012 PLEBISCITE WAS NOT A LEGITIMATE EXERCISE OF SELF-DETERMINATION

On November 6, 2012, the day of the general elections, voters were given a ballot with two questions that read as follows:

First Question:

Do you agree that Puerto Rico should continue to have its present form of territorial status? (Emphasis added).

Yes____ No____

Second Question:

Regardless of your selection in the first question, please mark which of the following non-territorial options you prefer.

Statehood: Puerto Rico should be admitted as a state of the United States of America so that all United States citizens residing in Puerto Rico may have rights, benefits, and responsibilities equal to those enjoyed by all other citizens of the states of the Union, and be entitled to full representation in Congress and to participate in the Presidential elections, and the United States Congress would be required to pass any necessary legislation to begin the transition into Statehood.

If you agree, place a mark here____.

Independence: Puerto Rico should become a sovereign nation, fully independent from the United States and Congress would be required to pass any necessary legislation to begin the transition into the independent nation of Puerto Rico.

If you agree, place a mark here____.

Sovereign Free Associated State (Estado Libre Asociado Soberano): Puerto Rico should adopt a status outside of the Territorial Clause of the United States Constitution that recognizes the sovereignty of the People of Puerto Rico. The Sovereign Free Associated State would be based on a free and voluntary association, the specific terms of which shall be agreed upon between the United States and Puerto Rico as sovereign nations. Such agreement would provide the scope of the jurisdictional powers that the People of Puerto Rico agree to confer to the United States and retain all other jurisdictional power and authorities.

If you agree, place a mark here___.

The pro-Commonwealth Popular Democratic Party opposed this plebiscite based on three main facts: (1) the process' biased structure, (2) the unfair characterization of the Commonwealth option, and (3) the disenfranchisement of pro-Commonwealth voters. This was an electoral process rigged in favor of statehood.

A. The plebiscite's structure was rigged in favor of statehood

The plebiscite's structure closely followed the process proposed in H.R. 2499 (111th Congress) by Resident Commissioner Pedro Pierluisi in 2009. H.R. 2499 only differed in that it called for the two separate votes to occur on different dates, holding the second vote only if the status quo was defeated in the first round. (And if the status quo won, the bill would subject it to continuous periodic voting.)

This structure was severely criticized on the House Floor. The Congressional Record shows that criticisms of H.R. 2499 in its original form came from both sides of the aisle and focused mainly on the exclusion of the Commonwealth option in the second vote.

As a result of those objections, the bill was amended to include the Commonwealth as an option in the second ballot and passed.

Revealingly, on May 20, 2010 Resident Commissioner Pierluisi came before this very Committee and acknowledged the fairness of the amendment:

> I should note something. When I introduced this bill originally I did not have that fourth option, the current status. My thinking as a lawyer was like, I was being logical in the sense if the majority of the people reject the current status, why include it in the second—the second time around? But I have to say now on behalf of my federal colleagues in the House, the sentiment in the House was let's make sure that nobody's left out, nobody who wants to support a valid option. And the current status called the Commonwealth, it is one option. We've been living through it for a long time.

Former Governor Luis Fortuño, did so as well:

> If a second stage vote does take place the current status will stand equally alongside the other possible status alternatives that are so important in Puerto Rico.

The 111th Congress ended without Senate action on H.R. 2499. The pro-statehood Puerto Rico legislature and Governor vowed to legislate it locally but delayed any action in anticipation of the White House Task Force Report on Puerto Rico's Status, released on March 16, 2011.

The report gave them a very strong admonition:

> To move forward, it is critical that the process is accepted by the people of Puerto Rico as fair and that it ensures that even those whose status option is not selected feel fairly treated. (White House Task Force Report on Puerto Rico's Status, p. 26)

Expressing such a concern is unusual, for fairness as a procedural specification should go without saying. Evidently, the Task Force felt that need. President Obama himself, during his visit to Puerto Rico in June of 2011, reiterated that warning: "The most important thing is that there is a sense of legitimacy to the process here in Puerto Rico." (Univision TV interview.)

H.R. 2499, in its original form, led to these admonitions. On this, the Task Force pointed out:

> In the original form of the bill, if a majority voted for a different political status, the people of Puerto Rico would then have another plebiscite to vote on three options: (1) Statehood; (2) Independence; or (3) Free Association. There was criticism that, under H.R. 2499 in its original form, if a change of status won the first vote but the vote was close, the second vote would not include an option that perhaps 49 percent of the population supported as a first option and an unspecified number believed was the second best option. In part, for this reason, those supporting certain options objected to the bill, and, as a result, it was amended to include a fourth option in the second plebiscite: the current political status. (Report, pp. 27-28.)

The then ruling pro-statehood legislature and Governor of Puerto Rico disregarded the concerns of both the House and the White House, and disregarded what they told this Committee. The inclusion of the Commonwealth option in the second round was not given serious consideration by the legislative assembly. All the rhetoric about "not leaving anybody out" or Commonwealth "standing equally alongside the other alternatives" was not sincere. This is the typical behavior of a statehood party that speaks about fairness in Congress but acts unfairly in Puerto Rico.

The Task Force Report had recommended a two round vote where the Puerto Ricans would first answer whether they preferred to remain part of the United States or separate, and then a run-off between the alternatives that fell under the winning category, Commonwealth and statehood would be the "in-union" options, independence, and free-association the "in-separation" ones. In contrast to the manner the statehood party handled this matter, I, then a senator in the minority party, introduced legislation adopting the Task Force's recommendations.

The two-question structure sought to conceal the fact that Commonwealth is still the preferred option among Puerto Ricans. In the 1993 plebiscite, Commonwealth got 48.6% of the vote, statehood 46.3% and independence 4.4%. Commonwealth won, although it did not pass the 50% mark. Those same results under the 2012 plebiscite structure, would have meant a Commonwealth defeat.

The results, nonetheless, show that statehood is on the decline and suggest that Commonwealth is still the preferred option.

A full-page ad published earlier this year in Politico by a pro-statehood group claimed that "over 75% of registered voters came to the polls, and 61% voted for statehood." That is a great example of how you can lie with numbers. You can only read that phrase one way; it is claiming that of those that "came to the polls," 61% voted for statehood. That is objectively false.

The Puerto Rico Elections Commission certified that 1,878,969 participated and that 834,191 voted for statehood. The truth is that of the total of votes cast, only 44.4% favor statehood.

The statehood group claims the number is 61%, but that is because they changed the manner in which the Elections Commission calculates percentages. Until this past plebiscite, percentages were calculated based on total ballots cast. The 2005 Report by the President's Task Force on Puerto Rico's Status calculated the 1993 result percentages based on total participation including blank and void ballots. Using that method, the Report states that statehood got 46.3% and 46.49% in those plebiscites. Statehooders recognize these percentages as valid.

However, the November 2012 plebiscite was the first election in which the Commission could no longer include blank and void ballots when calculating percentages. When blank and void ballots are excluded, the statehood percentage jumps from 44.4% to 61%. There has not been a surge in statehood support, just a change in how votes are counted or, should I say, excluded.

B. The plebiscite ballot had a serious language problem

i-The plebiscite did not refer to Commonwealth by its name

The Committee should wonder why the Puerto Rico legislature chose not to refer to the Commonwealth option in the ballot by its rightful and legal name, as used more than one thousand times in the US code, but instead used a derogatory "present form of territorial status."

The reference to Commonwealth as "present form of territorial status" was meant to offend its supporters and deter them from voting "Yes". This is sometimes overlooked in Washington where the term "territory" is used in a more general sense as an umbrella term that includes all US non-state entities. A memo from the Clinton years regarding "Mutual Consent Provisions in the Guam Commonwealth Legislation" acknowledges, in the first footnote, the pejorative sense that the term "territory" carries:

> Territories that have developed from the stage of a classical territory to that of a Commonwealth with a constitution of their own adoption and an elective governor, resent being called Territories and claim that that legal term and its implications are not applicable to them. We therefore shall refer to all Territories and Commonwealths as non-state areas under the sovereignty of the United States or briefly as non-state areas.

> In the particular case of Puerto Rico, the United States Code recognizes that:

> Fully recognizing the principle of government by consent, sections 731b to 731e of this title are now adopted in the nature of a compact so that the people of Puerto Rico may organize a government pursuant to a constitution of their own adoption. 48 U.S.C. §731b.

Those who seek to justify using the "present form of territorial status" terminology resort to the case of Nat. Bank v. County of Yankton, 101 U.S. 129, 133 (1879), for the proposition that "[a]ll territory within the jurisdiction of the United States not included in any state must necessarily be governed by or under the authority of the Congress." But that only reveals their ill-intent. County of Yankton reflects nineteenth century a state of mind, when the United States was expanding westward and incorporating territories for eventual statehood. It was understood that the Constitution provided for Congress to hold plenary powers over those territories until admission as a state. Two decades after Yankton County, however, the United States began to acquire territories not intended for eventual statehood. Through the years and decades, these new territories would evolve, to use the Clinton administration's terminology, from "classic territories" into other forms of relationship. Felix Frankfurter recognized this as far back as 1914 when he was a law officer in the U.S. Department of War:

> The form of the relationship between the United States and [an] unincorporated territory is solely a problem of statesmanship. History suggests a great diversity of relationships between a central government and [a] dependent territory. The present day shows a great variety in actual operation. One of the great demands upon creative statesmanship is to help evolve new kinds of relationship[s] so as to combine the advantages of local self-government with those of a confederated union. Luckily, our Constitution has left this field of invention open. The decisions in the Insular cases mean this, if they mean anything; that there is nothing in the Constitution to hamper the responsibility of Congress in working out, step by step, forms of government for our Insular possessions responsive to the largest needs and capacities of their inhabitants, and ascertained by the best wisdom of Congress.

Constitutional law has evolved to create this type of creative statesmanship. In the case of Puerto Rico, the United States Supreme Court recognized the change in the nature of the relationship between the United States and Puerto Rico that occurred in 1952:

> By 1950. . . pressures for greater autonomy led to congressional enactment of Pub. L. 600, 64 Stat. 319, which offered the people of Puerto Rico a compact whereby they might establish a government under their own constitution. Puerto Rico accepted the compact, and on July 3, 1952 Congress approved, with minor amendments, a constitution adopted by the Puerto Rican populace [...] Pursuant to that constitution the Commonwealth now "elects its Governor and legislature; appoints its judges, all cabinet officials, and lesser officials in the executive branch; sets its own educational policies; determines its own budget; and amends its own civil and criminal code." (citing Leibowitz, The Applicability of Federal Law to the Commonwealth of Puerto Rico, 56 GEO. L. J. 219, 221 (1967)).[1]

The Court then provided a general sense of what Puerto Rico had become with the transformation of its status from that of a mere territory into a Commonwealth by quoting at length, and with approval, from Chief Judge Magruder's observations in Mora v. Mejías:

> Puerto Rico has thus not become a State in the federal Union like the 48 States, but it would seem to have become a State within a common and accepted meaning of the word . . . It is a political entity created by the act and with the consent of the people of Puerto Rico and joined in union with the United States of America under the terms of the compact.[2]

The process followed for Puerto Rico in 1952 resembled that of the admission of States, with the adoption of a constitution and assumption by Puerto Rico of all responsibilities of local government. Unlike regular laws or organic acts, here an act of Congress came into effect only after the people of Puerto Rico gave their consent, therein its nature as a compact.

Two years later, the Court explained that "the purpose of Congress in the 1950 and 1952 legislation was to accord to Puerto Rico the degree of autonomy and independence normally associated with States of the Union [. . .]."[3] The Court reasoned, moreover, that through the establishment of the Commonwealth, "Congress relinquished its control over the organization of the local affairs of the island and granted Puerto Rico a measure of autonomy comparable to that possessed by the States." The Supreme Court describes the 1950-52 process as an act of relinquishment and

---

[1] Calero Toledo v. Pearson Yacht Leasing Co., 416 U.S. 663 (1974).
[2] Mora v. Mejias, 206 F.2d 377 (1st Cir. 1953).
[3] Examining Board v. Flores de Otero, 426 U.S. 572 (1976).

not as a mere delegation of powers. To "delegate" means "to entrust" which is inherently reversible. To "relinquish" is "to cease," which denotes irreversibility.

The concept of "relinquishment" in the territorial policy context appears earlier in the memorandum by then Assistant Attorney General William H. Rehnquist:

> [T]he Constitution does not inflexibly determine the incidents of territorial status, i.e., that Congress must necessarily have the unlimited and plenary power to legislate over it. Rather, Congress can gradually relinquish those powers and give what was once a Territory an ever-increasing measure of self-government. Such legislation could create vested rights of a political nature, hence it would bind future Congresses and cannot be "taken backward" unless by mutual agreement.[4]

In 1980 the U.S. Supreme Court issued a brief per curiam opinion in Harris v Rosario, stating that Congress could, under the Territory Clause, treat Puerto Rico differently in the application of the Aid to Families with Dependent Children program.[5] The case has often been misread as negating the Court's previous—and posterior—assertions that Puerto Rico has attained sovereignty similar to that of the States over its local affairs and as a snub to the claim that the relationship is based on a compact. But the case has nothing to do with any of that. It holds that generally Congress may treat Puerto Rico differently from the States if it has a rational basis to do so. But that pertains strictly to matters that fall under the federal sphere of powers, in that particular case to a federal assistance program.

Some claim that Harris v. Rosario shows that Puerto Rico is still a territory of the United States and, thus, that using the tag is appropriate. That debate is more semantic than substantial.

There is no contradiction between Congress having power under the Territory Clause and those powers being limited by compact. This was squarely addressed by the Ninth Circuit in the context of the Commonwealth of the Northern Mariana Islands, by saying: "Even if the Territorial Clause provides the constitutional basis for Congress' legislative authority in the Commonwealth, it is solely by the Covenant that we measure the limits of Congress' legislative power."[6]

The U.S. Supreme Court has long recognized that Congress can limit or restrict its powers under the Territory Clause. In Cincinnati Soap Co. v. U.S., the Court addressed the nature of the changes in status of the Philippine Islands upon the approval and adoption of a constitution for the Commonwealth of the Philippine Islands. The Court recognized that "these acts have brought about a profound change in the status of the islands and in their relations to the United States" and acknowledged that the power of the United States over the new Commonwealth had been so modified.[7]

Whatever confusion Harris may have provoked regarding the nature of the Commonwealth relationship was addressed by the Court in Rodriguez v. Popular Democratic Party, where it unambiguously stated that: "Puerto Rico, like a state, is an autonomous political entity, 'sovereign over matters not ruled by the Constitution.'"[8] The Court in Rodriguez cited with approval from Cordova & Simonpietri Ins. Agency Inc. v. Chase Manhattan Bank N.A., a decision authored by then Circuit Judge, and now Supreme Court Justice, Stephen Breyer. Cordova seminally sums up the nature of the Commonwealth relationship:

> [In 1952] Puerto Rico's status changed from that of a mere territory to the unique status of Commonwealth. And the federal government's relations with Puerto Rico changed from being bounded merely by the territorial clause, and the rights of the people of Puerto Rico as United States citizens, to being bounded by the United States and Puerto Rico Constitutions, Public Law 600, the Puerto Rican Federal Relations Act and the rights of the people of Puerto Rico as United States citizens.[9]

When adopted, the Commonwealth of Puerto Rico was hailed as major example of that creativity. Chief Justice Earl Warren, in a speech given in 1956 on the occasion of the inauguration of the new Puerto Rico Supreme Court Building, put it eloquently:

---

[4] Re: Micronesian Negotiations (Office of Legal Counsel, Aug. 18, 1971).
[5] Harris v. Rosario, 446 U.S. 651 (1980).
[6] U.S. ex rel. Richards v. De León Guerrero, 4 F.3d 749 (9th Cir. 1993).
[7] Cincinnati Soap Co. v. U.S., 301 U.S. 308 (1937).
[8] Rodriguez v. Popular Democratic Party, 457 U.S. 1 (1982).
[9] Cordova & Simonpietri Ins. Agency Inc. v. Chase Manhattan Bank N.A., 649 F. 2d 36, 39-42 (1st Cir. 1981).

In the sense that our American system is not static, in the sense that it is not an end but the means to an end; in the sense that it is an organism intended to grow and expand to meet varying conditions and items in a large country; in the sense that every governmental effort of ours is an experiment-so the new institutions of the Commonwealth of Puerto Rico represent an experiment—the newest experiment and perhaps the most notable of American governmental experiments in our lifetimes.[10]

The reference to the Commonwealth of Puerto Rico as "present form of territorial status" in the ballot was ill intended. It sought to deny the achievements of the compact created by the United States and Puerto Rico in 1952

ii. The plebiscite disenfranchised pro-Commonwealth voters because it failed to recognize the possibility of an enhanced Commonwealth

Referring to the Commonwealth as territorial in nature is only part of the problem. From its inception, the Commonwealth concept has always been conceived as a dynamic relationship subject to development and growth. However, the 2012 ballot limited the Commonwealth option to its "current" form only, thus excluding from the ballot those who believe that the best option for Puerto Rico is a further developed form of Commonwealth. This option appeared in the 1967 and 1993 plebiscites and won. What happened in 2012 was the disenfranchisement of pro-Commonwealth voters.

The establishment of the Commonwealth status was undoubtedly a significant achievement. Until then, no territory or possession had been allowed to adopt is own constitution and elect its own governor and legislature. Until then, Congress had delegated to some extent the administration or governance of local affairs to territories through organic acts, but it had not relinquished those powers and granted state-like sovereignty.

The creation of the Commonwealth of Puerto Rico was not the culmination of an innovative process of self-determination and US federalism. From the very beginning, Commonwealth adherents recognized the need to address certain issues. One of these issues was the applicability of certain Federal Laws in Puerto Rico. For instance, under this innovative relationship nothing prevents Congress and Puerto Rico from agreeing on mechanisms for the exemption of Puerto Rico from specific Federal laws and wherein the Commonwealth is authorized to submit to the United States proposals for the entry of Puerto Rico into international agreements, in order that Puerto Rico may govern matters necessary to its economic, social, and cultural development.

Puerto Rico's first elected governor and main architect of the Commonwealth, Luis Muñoz Marín, in a letter to President Kennedy wrote the following:

In planning the growth of the Commonwealth, we should, I believe, proceed along the following lines:

(1) The indispensable principle of the Commonwealth is self-government for Puerto Rico in permanent association with the United States on the basis of common loyalty, common citizenship, mutual dedication to democracy and mutual commitment to freedom.

(2) The moral and juridical basis of the Commonwealth should be further clarified so as to eliminate any possible basis for the accusation, which is made by enemies and misguided friends of the United States and Puerto Rico, that the Commonwealth was not the free choice of the people of Puerto Rico acting in their sovereign capacity, but was merely a different kind of colonial arrangement to which they consented.

(3) The governmental power and authority of the Commonwealth should be complete and any reservations or exceptions which are not an indispensable part of the arrangements for permanent association with the United States should be eliminated. Methods should be devised for forms of participation, appropriate to the Commonwealth concept, by the people of Puerto Rico on federal functions that affect them.

Certainly, the interests of the United States and of Puerto Rico would be greatly served by reaffirmation of our compact—including the guarantees of permanent association and common citizenship which practically all Puerto Ricans prize deeply—in a form which will leave no room for doubt as to the sovereign capacity of the people of Puerto Rico to give and receive these commitments.

---

[10] Speech on the occasion of the inauguration of the new Puerto Rico Supreme Court Building, 1956.

In response to Muñoz's letter, President Kennedy said: "I am aware, as you point out, that the Commonwealth relationship is not perfected and that it has not yet realized its full potential. . .I am in full sympathy with this aspiration."

Since 1952 there have been several efforts, taking various forms, to further develop Commonwealth. Three merit discussion for they show that a further development of Commonwealth status is a matter of political will and statesmanship.

(i) 94th Congress: The New Compact.—In October, 1975, an Ad Hoc Advisory Group on Puerto Rico appointed by President Nixon and Governor Hernández Colón presented a "Compact of Permanent Union Between Puerto Rico and the United States." The Advisory Group included U.S. Senators and Members of Congress, the founder of the Commonwealth of Puerto Rico and former Governor, Luis Muñoz Marín, and a number of other distinguished individuals from the U.S and Puerto Rico. The proposed compact was the result of a process of studies, inquiries, public hearings, reports and discussions over a two-year period.

The group concluded that:

> It must be noted finally that the relationship between Puerto Rico and the United States since its inception in 1898, and especially since 1950-1952, has been unique within the American Federal system. However, because this association is unique and exists within a dynamic social and economic system, much debate has surrounded it during the twenty-three years since the Puerto Rican Constitution was adopted. Public Law 600 primarily recognized the right of self-government by the people of Puerto Rico and established the process by which their representatives, freely and specifically elected for that purpose, drafted a constitution which the people of Puerto Rico adopted.

> Public Law 600 and the Constitution of Puerto Rico were noteworthy advances in the progress toward the maximum of self-government and self-determination by the people of Puerto Rico. However, Public Law 600 retained an accumulation of previous statutory provisions. These included several provisions from the Foraker Act of 1900, which established the first political and economic association between the United States and Puerto Rico after its cession from Spain to the United States in 1898. Also many were retained from the Jones Act of 1917 and some from the Elective Governor's Act of 1947. The Jones Act of 1917 improved the political relationship, bestowed United States citizenship on the people of Puerto Rico, and retained ultimate Congressional control over Puerto Rico. This accumulation of provisions is in many ways anachronic. It is the belief of the Advisory Group on Puerto Rico that the time is appropriate to draft a new compact as a substitute for the Federal Relations Act.

The proposed new compact would define Commonwealth as follows:

> The people of Puerto Rico constitute an autonomous body politic organized by their own, free and sovereign will and in common agreement with the United States under the juridical structure and official name of the Free Associated State of Puerto Rico . . . The right of the Free Associated State of Puerto Rico to govern itself is hereby recognized as well as the right to exercise all the necessary powers and authority to govern the people of Puerto Rico according to its own Constitution and laws and to make a compact with the United States as to the nature of its present and future political relations . . . In order to respect the right of self government guaranteed by this compact, the United States agrees that the provisions of this Compact may be modified only by mutual agreement between the government of the United States and the government of the Free Associated State of Puerto Rico." [Arts 1, 2, 21 New Compact]

The proposed "New Compact" dealt with matters such as legal title to lands and navigable waters, citizenship, internal revenue, immigration, representation (proposing one non-voting representative in the Senate in addition to the one it has since 1900 in the House of Representatives), assignment of federal functions to Puerto Rico (if Puerto Rico agrees to assume the "expenses and responsibilities"), labor, and the environment.

The proposal further provided a solution to one of Commonwealth's most vexing problems: the automatic application of federal laws to Puerto Rico. The compact proposed an objection mechanism wherein Puerto Rico could protest the application of a given legislation triggering a process whereby Congress, following certain criteria, could exclude Puerto Rico from the application of a given law. While this has always been contemplated as an exceptional mechanism that would be used very sparingly, it helps resolve the current democratic fault of having the governed automatically ruled by laws adopted without their participation. Regarding this proposal for an enhanced Commonwealth, then Acting Assistant Attorney General for Legislative Affairs, A. Mitchell McConnell, Jr., commented:

> The proposed Compact would, without altering the fundamental nature of Puerto Rico's Commonwealth status, provide substantially increased autonomy to the island government and its people . . . Such autonomy may be granted to Puerto Rico because Congress under the Constitution (Article IV, § 3) has plenary power over the territories of the United States and Puerto Rico remains a territory as that word is used in the Constitution. Cf. Detres v. Lions Building Corp., 234 F. 2d 596 (7th Cir. 1956). In this light, it is possible for Congress to bind future Congresses with respect to Puerto Rico by means of a "compact." This may be viewed either as the vesting of certain rights, see, e.g., Downes v. Bidwell, 182 US 244, 261-71 (1901), or as the granting of a certain measure of independence which once granted cannot be retrieved. Thus, specifically, Article 21 of the proposed Compact, requiring mutual agreement for amendment of the Compact, would, in our belief, be constitutional. Indeed, its explicit statement would appear to be an improvement over the situation under the present Compact where there is some question as to the ability of Congress to change its provisions.[11]

A bill incorporating the compact was introduced in the House, H.R. 11200 (approved in subcommittee), and Senate, S. Res. 215, but the Commonwealth party's defeat in the 1976 elections for reasons unrelated to the status issue, put an end to such effort.

(ii) H.R. 4765, 101th Congress.—Another significant effort to enhance Commonwealth occurred during the 101th Congress, where the House of Representatives unanimously passed H.R. 4765, a bill calling for a plebiscite on status. The House Report on the bill included the following definition of a "New Commonwealth":

> A NEW COMMONWEALTH RELATIONSHIP.—(A) The new Commonwealth of Puerto Rico would be joined in a union with the United States that would be permanent and the relationship could only be altered by mutual consent. Under a compact, the Commonwealth would be an autonomous body politic with its own character and culture, not incorporated into the United States, and sovereign over matters governed by the Constitution of Puerto Rico, consistent with the Constitution of the United States.

> (B) The United States citizenship of persons born in Puerto Rico would be guaranteed and secured as provided by the Fifth Amendment of the Constitution of the United States and equal to that of citizens born in the several States. The individual rights, privileges, and immunities provided for by the Constitution of the United States would apply to residents of Puerto Rico. Residents of Puerto Rico would be entitled to receive benefits under Federal social programs equally with residents of the several States contingent on equitable contributions from Puerto Rico as provided by law.

> (C) To enable Puerto Rico to govern matters necessary to its economic, social, and cultural development under its constitution, the Commonwealth would be authorized to submit proposals for the entry of Puerto Rico into international agreements or the exemption of Puerto Rico from specific Federal laws or provisions thereof to the United States. The President and the Congress, as appropriate, would consider whether such proposals would be consistent with the vital national interests of the United States on an expedited basis through special procedures to be provided by law. The Commonwealth would assume any expenses related to increased responsibilities resulting from the approval of these proposals.

As with the 1975 compact proposal, this definition of New Commonwealth provided for the "exemption of Puerto Rico from federal laws and for the entry of Puerto Rico into international agreements, so long as the proposals are consistent with the vital national interests of the United States."

(iii) S. 224, 102nd Congress.—The Senate did not consider H.R. 4765. Instead, Senator Johnston, the Chairman of the Energy Committee, and Senator Wallop, the Ranking Minority Member, introduced their own bill, S.224, in the 102nd Congress. This bill also promoted a referendum in the various status alternatives, with a Com-

---

[11] A. Mitchell McConnell to Marlow W. Cook, Department of Justice, Washington, D.C. 12 May 1975.

monwealth definition that made explicit some of its characteristics and established its further enhancement as a policy of the United States:

SEC 401.PRINCIPLES OF COMMONWEALTH

a. The Commonwealth of Puerto Rico is a unique juridical status, created as a compact between the People of Puerto Rico and the United States, under which Puerto Rico enjoys sovereignty, like a State to the extent provided by the Tenth Amendment to the United States' Constitution and in addition with autonomy consistent with its character, culture and location. The relationship is permanent unless revoked by mutual consent.

b. The policy of the United States shall be to enhance the Commonwealth relationship enjoyed by the Commonwealth of Puerto Rico and the United States to enable the people of Puerto Rico to accelerate their economic and social development, to attain maximum cultural autonomy, to seek fair treatment in Federal programs, and in matters of government to take into account local conditions in Puerto Rico.

c. The United States citizenship of persons born in Puerto Rico shall continue to be guaranteed and indefeasible to the same extent as that of citizens born in the several states.

S.224 was defeated in mark up by members of the Energy Committee because some had objections to the inclusion of statehood as an option in the self-executing bill.[12] None had objections to the enhanced Commonwealth definition.

The U.S. Supreme Court has pointed out that "modify[ing] the degree of autonomy enjoyed by a dependent sovereign that is not a State—is not an unusual legislative objective."[13] History shows that Congress has engaged in far more radical adjustments to the autonomy of non-States (e.g. the Philippines) than those required for the enhanced Commonwealth formulations discussed above.

By failing to present the option of Commonwealth with enhancement potential, supporters of Commonwealth status were denied the opportunity to vote for their choice of association. They were unable to reiterate their desire that Puerto Rico continue to pursue enhancements of the Commonwealth for the benefit of both Puerto Rico and the United States.

iii-The plebiscite wrongful and ill-intentionally applied the term Commonwealth to the Free Association option

In Spanish, Commonwealth is known as Estado Libre Asociado, which translates literally to "Free Associated State". The term "Commonwealth" was chosen over "Free Associated State" because of its familiarity among members of Congress in 1952.

In the November plebiscite, while pro-statehood legislators avoided using the term Commonwealth in reference to the Commonwealth option itself, they unabashedly used the term in the ballot to denominate the free association option, calling it "Estado Libre Asociado Soberano" or "Sovereign Free Associated State." There are marked differences between the concepts of free association and Commonwealth. The U.S. defined both in the 1980s when it offered them to its protectorates in the Pacific. The Mariana Islands chose to become a Commonwealth while the Republic of Palau, Micronesia and the Marshall Islands chose free association.

Free association, as applied in those three cases, is a form of independence. Those compacts of association are for a specific term subject to renewal and renegotiation. The residents of the associated country are not U.S. citizens. In contrast, residents in a Commonwealth are citizens by birth and the compacts do not have an expiration date subject to renegotiation. Their sovereignty is not that of an independent nation but similar to that of the States.

The ballot's definition for "Sovereign Free Associated State" was that of free association. It specifically describes the relationship between the U.S. and Puerto Rico as between sovereign nations and makes no mention of U.S. citizenship.

During legislation, the statehood party fended off criticism that they were deliberately trying to confuse voters claiming that "Sovereign Free Associated State" was taken from the PDPs 2008 platform. "Sovereign Free Associated State" in such platform did not refer to an independent Puerto Rico in association with the U.S., as would be the case under free association and as asserted in the ballot. The term "sovereign," as used in the platform, referred to the relationship resulting from specific consent by the people of Puerto Rico.

---

[12] Senate Comm. On Energy and Natural Resources, 102d Cong, 1st Session, Business Meeting (February 20, 1991) and Business Meeting February 27, 1991.
[13] U.S. v. Lara, 541 U.S. 193, 203-04 (2004).

iv. The Popular Democratic Party voted in protest

The PDP charged the statehood party with deliberately stacking the deck against Commonwealth with the two question structure and seeking to exclude and divide Commonwealth supporters by manipulating the ballot's language.

In February 2012, the party's governing board passed a resolution recommending that voters disregard the reference to Commonwealth as the "present form of territorial status" and vote "yes" in the first question. Since Puerto Rico's Supreme Court recently stated that a blank ballot "expresses an inconformity with the presented proposals,"[14] the Party asked voters to leave the second question blank as a form of protest.

Some party leaders, including a former governor, argued that leaving a ballot blank was susceptible to fraud and would allow statehood supporters to claim an artificial victory with an inflated percentage. They openly recommended voting for "Sovereign Free Associated State," although under the pledge that it would not be interpreted as a vote for free association.

The unusually high number of blank ballots and votes for free association demonstrate an inconformity with the ballot. In the previous plebiscite, only 0.1% cast blank ballots and 0.3% for free association. That is less than half of a percentage point combined. But in the November plebiscite, 26.5% cast blank ballots and 24.2% voted for free association. Combined, their numbers rose from 0.4% in the previous plebiscite to 50.7%. One could disingenuously interpret that as a massive shift in voter preference. But the most reasonable explanation is that those were the two options where Commonwealth supporters sought refuge.

II. WE ARE OPTIMISTIC ABOUT THE ADMINISTRATION'S EFFORTS

The Administration has recommended an appropriation of:

> $2,500,000 for objective, nonpartisan voter education about, and a plebiscite on, options that would resolve Puerto Rico's future political status, which shall be provided to the State Elections Commission of Puerto Rico.

The appropriation includes several provisions:

> Provided, that funds provided for the plebiscite under the previous provision shall not be obligated until 45 days after the Attorney General notifies the Committees on Appropriations that he approves of an expenditure plan from the Commission for voter education and plebiscite administration, including approval of the plebiscite ballot;

> Provided further, that the notification shall include a finding that the voter education materials, plebiscite ballot, and related materials are not incompatible with the Constitution and laws and policies of the United States.

While under normal circumstances the Department of Justice's participation in this process is unnecessary—historically this type of referenda have been conducted locally—there are at least two justifications for the Department of Justice's involvement this time around. One is the mistrust caused by all matters surrounding the last plebiscite. Two, while the Department of Justice's involvement is not legally a commitment to the results, I understand the President would become morally obligated to support the result.

Some claim that the language in the budget proposal that says "not incompatible with the Constitution and laws and policies of the United States" is a reference to precluding the enhanced commonwealth concept. This is not the case. There is no blanket rejection there, but rather an assurance that the "enhanced commonwealth" proposal that ends up in the ballot is constitutionally viable.

That becomes clear when read in conjunction with Report by the President's Task Force on Puerto Rico's Status, published on March 2011.

On page 32, the report addresses some areas of enhancement that are not constitutionally problematic, and that Puerto Rico would need to negotiate with Congress:

> If they selected Commonwealth, would Congress enact legislation to define what, if any, possible changes could be made to the Commonwealth status? Advocates for increases in Puerto Rican autonomy within the Commonwealth framework have argued for congressional legislation that would establish a process by which Puerto Rico could obtain relief from specific Federal laws, or enhance authority for the government of Puerto Rico to

---

[14] Suárez Cáceres v. Comisión Estatal de Elecciones, 176 D. P.R. 31 (2009)

join certain international organizations and to engage in international cultural and economic outreach efforts so long as such activities were authorized by the Federal Government as consistent with the foreign relations of the United States. When the people of Puerto Rico vote among the status options, they should not assume such modifications unless legislation specifically provides that such a modification would occur upon selection of that status.

Since the Administration has not expressed an objection to enhanced Commonwealth per se, only to some aspects of it, we welcome the opportunity of discussing the enhancement potential of the Commonwealth with the Department of Justice.

In sum, I am optimistic that the Administration and Congress will act in a fair and balanced manner. I hope that the proposal put forth by the President is an opportunity to hold a plebiscite that is transparent, democratic and respectful of all self-determination options, including the pursuit of a more perfect compact between the United States and the Commonwealth.

The CHAIRMAN. Governor, thank you very much.

Let's go next to the Resident Commissioner Pierluisi.

Mr. Pierluisi and Commissioner, please proceed.

STATEMENT OF HON. PEDRO R. PIERLUISI, RESIDENT COMMISSIONER TO CONGRESS, PUERTO RICO, AND PRESIDENT OF THE NEW PROGRESSIVE PARTY

Mr. PIERLUISI. Chairman Wyden, Ranking Member Murkowski, Senator Heinrich, Senator Flake, I am particularly pleased to see my former colleagues here serving in the Senate. I'm glad to address the committee on this important issue.

Last November Puerto Rico held a free and fair vote on its political status. The ballot had two questions.

Voters were first asked if they want Puerto Rico to remain a territory and 54 percent said no while 46 percent said yes.

I have the official certification of the State Elections Commission of Puerto Rico to confirm this.

A party in Puerto Rico, the PDP urged a yes vote. Nevertheless, voters rejected territory status by a wide margin. The current status has now lost its Democratic legitimacy to the extent that the people of Puerto Rico ever consented to this status, such consent has been withdrawn.

This result should not be surprising. I represent more U.S. citizens than 42 Senators. My constituents have fought side by side with your constituents from Korea to Afghanistan. They can move to the states for the price of a plane ticket. But if they stay in Puerto Rico they cannot vote for President, have no representation in the Senate and elect one member to the House.

I can only watch as my colleagues cast Floor votes on bills affecting every aspect of life on the island. I depend on the good will of Senators elected to protect the interest of their constituents, not mine. I request assistance from a President who is not required to earn a vote in Puerto Rico.

To expect a Presidential Administration to feel the same obligation to support Puerto Rico as it does the states is to substitute hope for experience. The failure of the current Administration to send the witness to testify today is a sad reminder of this point.

Moreover, territory status gives the Federal Government license to discriminate against Puerto Rico. The island is treated unfairly under numerous Federal laws including most safety net programs.

There is consensus that territory status is the root cause of the economic problems that have persisted in Puerto Rico for at least 4 decades. The best evidence that the status quo has failed is this, in the brief period from 2004 to 2012, Puerto Rico's population decreased by 4.2 percent with hundreds of thousands of residents leaving for the states in search of improved quality of life.

I turn now to the second question in the referendum which asked voters to express their preference among the 3 valid alternatives to the current status. Of those who chose an option, 61 percent voted for statehood. The State Elections Commission so certifies as well.

For the first time ever, this is important. For the first time ever, the number of votes for statehood exceeded the number of votes for the current status.

Before the vote the PDP complained that the second question was unfair because it did not include its status proposal, known as enhanced Commonwealth. Party leaders urged voters to leave the question blank and some did. They now cite this abstention as the basis for their argument that statehood, somehow, lost the vote.

That is nonsense.

Self determination is a choice among options that can be implemented not an exercise in wishful thinking. The PDP's proposal has been repeatedly rejected by Federal officials including this committee on legal and policy grounds. Therefore, it could not have appeared on the ballot.

Ultimately, those blank ballots do nothing to detract from the main point which is that a majority of voters reject territory status. A super majority favors statehood among the alternatives. More voters want statehood than any other status option.

No Senator would accept territory status for their constituents. So you must respect that my constituents do not accept it either.

With my support the Administration requested an appropriation to conduct the federally authorized status vote in the territory's history. With a declared goal of resolving the issue that funding was approved by the House Appropriations Committee confirming that the effort to secure justice for Puerto Rico is not and should not be a partisan issue. For Puerto Rico to resolve its ultimate status it must become a State or a sovereign Nation either independent from or in association with the U.S.

Territory status should not be an option because it has failed. An enhanced Commonwealth cannot be an option because it is fiction.

I have filed legislation that outlines the rights and responsibilities of statehood provides for an up or down vote in Puerto Rico on the territory's admission as a State and prescribes the steps the Federal Government would take if statehood obtains the majority. Those supporting statehood and those opposing it would have equal opportunity to express their views.

My bill already has 105 co-sponsors. It is my hope that a Senator will introduce a companion bill that U.S. citizens of Puerto Rico deserve. Now they have demanded it, a Democratic and dignified status. Congress must take action.

Thank you.

[The prepared statement of Mr. Pierluisi follows:]

PREPARED STATEMENT OF HON. PEDRO R. PIERLUISI, RESIDENT COMMISSIONER TO CONGRESS, PUERTO RICO, AND PRESIDENT OF THE NEW PROGRESSIVE PARTY

Chairman Wyden, Ranking Member Murkowski, and Members of the Committee: Thank you for inviting me to testify about the status referendum Puerto Rico held last November, and about the federal government's response.

To summarize, the results of the referendum demonstrate that a solid majority of the U.S. citizens of Puerto Rico want to end the island's current status as a territory; that a supermajority prefer statehood among the three possible alternatives to the current status; and that more voters favor statehood than any other status option, including the current status. The Administration responded by proposing a $2.5 million appropriation to conduct the first federally-sponsored status vote in Puerto Rico's history, to be held among one or more options that would "resolve" the territory's future status. The House Appropriations Committee has approved that proposal. In addition, I introduced bipartisan legislation in the House—cosponsored by over 100 of my colleagues—that proceeds from the irrefutable premise that statehood obtained more votes than any other status option in the November referendum. The bill, H.R. 2000, outlines the rights and responsibilities of statehood, provides for an up-or-down vote on statehood, and prescribes the steps that the president and Congress would take in the event of a majority vote for statehood. Those who support statehood and those who oppose it will have equal opportunity to express their views. Reduced to its essence, the message I want to convey to the Committee is this: On November 6th, Puerto Rico withdrew its consent to territory status. The federal government must respect—and respond to—the democratically expressed will of its own citizens.

***

Status is the central issue in Puerto Rico's political life. One party, the New Progressive Party, or PNP, favors statehood. Another party, the Puerto Rico Independence Party, or PIP, supports independence.

The third party, the Popular Democratic Party, or PDP, prefers the current status to either statehood or independence. At the same time, the PDP champions a proposal that its leaders often describe as an "enhanced" version of the current status, but that is in fact fundamentally different than the current status. This proposal has been repeatedly rejected by federal officials in the executive and legislative branches on both constitutional and policy grounds, including by former Committee Chairman Jeff Bingaman and Ranking Member Murkowski in a December 2010 letter to President Obama.

I am honored to speak on behalf of the U.S. citizens from Puerto Rico who seek equal rights and equal responsibilities through statehood, a status we believe would be in the best interest of both Puerto Rico and the United States. The PNP is unique among the island's parties because it draws support from across the political spectrum, from liberal Democrats to conservative Republicans. The goal of the PNP is to perfect our union with the United States, rather than to dilute or dissolve the bonds we have forged over the past 115 years. I view the struggle for statehood as a fight for civil and political rights, economic progress, and a better standard of living for the people I represent. The fact that this aspiration is not universally shared in Puerto Rico does not diminish the nobility of the aspiration itself.

I appeared before this Committee in May 2010, when a hearing was held on my status bill, H.R. 2499, which had been approved by the House. During the hearing, Senator Murkowski noted: "As someone who was born in Alaska when we were still a territory, I do have great sympathy for the desire of the people of Puerto Rico to resolve their political status. It took Alaska 92 years. . . . Puerto Rico has been working on it for 112." Senator Murkowski also noted that the process to determine Alaska's future was "driven from Alaska, not from Washington, DC," and expressed her view that the same should hold true for Puerto Rico.

I agree—and I want to underscore that Puerto Rico is, indeed, driving this process. In December 2011, the duly elected government of Puerto Rico enacted a local law providing for a status referendum to be held. Several million dollars in public funds were spent to support voter outreach and to administer the referendum. On November 6, 2012, a free and fair vote was conducted, with turnout exceeding 75 percent of registered voters. The results of the vote were certified by the Puerto Rico Elections Commission and transmitted to the President and Congress. All of this took place at Puerto Rico's initiative.

***

The referendum consisted of two questions. The first question asked voters if they want Puerto Rico to maintain its current territory status. Puerto Rico is an unincorporated territory of the United States, subject to Congress's broad powers under the Territory Clause of the U.S. Constitution. The term "unincorporated" indicates that Puerto Rico has the potential to become either a state or a sovereign nation. The federal government has enacted measures that, in the aggregate, have allowed Puerto Rico to exercise about the same degree of authority over its local affairs that the states are entitled to exercise under the Constitution. But these measures have not changed Puerto Rico's status, and Congress could rescind the autonomy it has delegated to Puerto Rico if it chose. Today's hearing is being held because this Committee has jurisdiction over "territorial policy . . . including changes in status."

Of the nearly 1.8 million voters who answered the first question, 970,910 voters—53.97 percent—voted "No" to maintaining the current territory status, while 828,077 voters—46.03 percent—voted "Yes." This is the official result certified by the Elections Commission, which consists of representatives from each of the territory's status-based parties.

There is no legitimate basis upon which to challenge the fairness or the outcome of the first question, and such efforts by PDP leaders do not survive even the slightest scrutiny. Moreover, there are 100 members of the U.S. Senate and 435 voting members of the U.S. House. None of you would accept territory status for your own constituents, so I know you will respect that my constituents do not accept it either.

***

Before turning to the second question on the referendum, I want to outline the three fundamental defects of territory status, because it is important to understand what the people of Puerto Rico rejected, and why they rejected it.

First, territory status deprives my constituents of political rights. I represent more U.S. citizens—3.6 million—than 42 senators. My constituents have fought shoulder-to-shoulder with your constituents, under the same flag, on battlefields from Korea and Vietnam to Iraq and Afghanistan. Residents of Puerto Rico can relocate from Puerto Rico to the states without any obstacle save the cost of a one-way plane ticket. But, if they choose to remain in Puerto Rico, they cannot vote for their president, have no representation in the Senate, and elect one member to the House—the Resident Commissioner—with limited voting rights. In the 21st century, in the most democratic nation on earth, this is astonishing. And it should be unacceptable.

Federal law is supreme in Puerto Rico, yet I can only watch as my House colleagues cast floor votes on bills that affect, for better or for worse, every aspect of life on the island. I must rely on the goodwill of senators like you. But you were elected to protect the interests of your constituents, not mine—so, understandably, our needs are not always your highest priority. I must request assistance from a president who is not obliged to seek or earn our vote. To expect the administration to feel the same urgency to produce positive results for Puerto Rico as it does for the states is to substitute hope for experience.

In addition, territory status gives the federal government a license to discriminate against Puerto Rico. It should come as no surprise, given our lack of political power, that the federal government often uses that license. Puerto Rico is excluded from—or treated unfairly under—various federal laws, including nearly every social safety-net program. The territory receives fewer federal funds per resident than any state or the District of Columbia. In 2010, Puerto Rico received about $5,300 per capita from the federal government, which is half the national average.

It has been argued that Puerto Rico should receive fewer federal funds than the states because territory residents are not required to pay federal taxes on their local income. Among its other deficiencies, this argument overlooks that residents of Puerto Rico pay all federal payroll taxes, that nearly half of all households in the states do not pay federal income taxes, and that—through refundable tax credits—federal law actually provides a substantial benefit to working families in the states that it denies to working families in Puerto Rico. To illustrate, consider a married couple with two children living in the states that earns $25,000, and then consider an identical family living in Puerto Rico. Both families owe the same payroll taxes. But the stateside family would receive over $6,000 in credits under the Earned Income Tax Credit and Child Tax Credit programs, for a final income of over $30,000. The Puerto Rico family, because it is ineligible for the EITC or the CTC, takes home less than $24,000. This is a useful example to bear in mind the next time you hear someone extol the supposed "advantages" of territory status.

.

Finally, territory status—and the unequal playing field it creates—has harmed Puerto Rico's economy and, therefore, quality of life on the island. Between 2004 and 2012, Puerto Rico's population decreased by 4.2 percent, nearly all through migration to the states. This is the sort of exodus that one typically sees only in the wake of a natural disaster. In the nearly 40 years that the federal government has published statistics, Puerto Rico's unemployment rate has averaged 15.5 percent, risen as high as 24 percent, and almost never dipped below 10 percent. At no point in time in the last 450 months has a state ever had an unemployment rate as high as Puerto Rico's. The data on household income reveal a similar pattern. Indeed, whatever economic metric we use, the numbers tell the same narrative: Puerto Rico has lagged far behind the states for at least four decades, and the gap is only increasing.

Political leaders in Puerto Rico, in an effort to spur economic activity, have generally resorted to a policy of offering tax and other incentives to large multinational corporations, but this policy has failed to produce substantial and sustained results. It is clear that territory status serves as a perpetual economic headwind, slowing or stopping forward progress by the ship of state, regardless of who is at the helm.

***

The second question on the referendum asked voters to express their preference among the three possible alternatives to territory status. The certified results show that, of the nearly 1.4 million voters who chose an option, 834,191 voters—61.16 percent—chose statehood, 33.34 percent chose nationhood in free association with the United States, and 5.49 percent chose independence. Of critical importance, the number of votes for statehood on the second question (834,191) exceeded the number of votes for the current status on the first question (828,077). For the first time in history, more voters in Puerto Rico want the territory to become a state than to continue its current status.

PDP leaders seek to downplay the result of the second question by noting that close to 500,000 voters did not provide an answer. In the run-up to the referendum, some PDP leaders encouraged voters to leave the second question blank, though other PDP leaders encouraged voters to choose the free association option, aware that blank ballots "shall not be deemed to be a vote cast" under Puerto Rico election law and general election practice. Although it is impossible to divine voter intent from a blank ballot, we can speculate that some—but by no means all—of the voters who did not answer the second question were responding to this appeal. If blank ballots are included in the vote total, the PDP's theory runs, statehood's supermajority victory becomes a plurality victory, though a victory nonetheless.

This argument is thin and, ultimately, beside the point. The purpose of the second question was to ascertain the voters' preference among the valid alternatives to territory status. And it is well-established that there are only three alternatives to territory status. Each of those options was included.

Nevertheless, PDP leaders continue to insist that the party's proposal—called "New Commonwealth" or "Enhanced Commonwealth"—should have been on the ballot. Simply to describe this proposal—which PDP leaders dutifully avoid doing in public—is to discredit it. Under this proposal, residents of Puerto Rico would retain their U.S. citizenship, and Puerto Rico would receive at least as much federal funding as it does now. In addition, Puerto Rico would be able to decide which federal laws apply on the island and to limit federal court jurisdiction, and to enter international organizations and international agreements as if it were a sovereign nation. Finally, Congress—once it agreed to this arrangement—could not modify its terms or withdraw without the consent of Puerto Rico.

In a March 2011 report, the Obama administration—concurring with the two prior administrations, former Chairman Bingaman and Ranking Member Murkowski, and the House Natural Resources Committee, among others—rejected the core of this proposal on constitutional grounds, reiterated that the only alternatives to territory status are statehood and nationhood, and confirmed that, under any "Commonwealth" proposal advanced by the PDP, "Puerto Rico would remain, as it is today, subject to the Territory Clause of the U.S. Constitution." Accordingly, to the extent that PDP leaders argue that the second question was unfair because it should have included their preferred status proposal, that argument is without merit.

In the final analysis, the fact that some voters left the answer to the second question blank does nothing to detract from the broader point, which is that a majority of voters in Puerto Rico do not support the current territory status, a supermajority favor statehood among the three valid alternatives, and more voters want statehood than any other option, including the current status. These results are now part of the historical record, and they cannot be dismissed or diminished by those who find them inconvenient.

***

Now that American citizens living in an American territory have informed the federal government, in a free and fair vote, that they do not consent to a political status that deprives them of the right to choose the leaders who make their national laws and the right to equal treatment under those laws, it is imperative that the federal government take steps to facilitate Puerto Rico's transition to a democratic and dignified status.

It is true that Puerto Rico should drive the self-determination process—and we are. But it is equally true that Congress has a constructive role to play in this process for both legal and moral reasons.

As a legal matter, the Constitution vests Congress with broad authority over its territories, including the power to decide whether, when and how to "dispose of" a territory. For Puerto Rico to become a state or sovereign nation, it is not enough for Puerto Rico to seek such a change; Congress—and the president—must act to enable that change.

As a moral matter, the federal government rightfully prides itself as a champion of democracy and self-determination around the world. It should—indeed, it must—adhere to those principles with respect to its own citizens.

I am encouraged by what I have seen to date, but believe that more needs to be done. In April, the Administration requested an appropriation of $2.5 million, which would be provided to the Puerto Rico Elections Commission to conduct the first federally authorized status vote in the territory's history, with the express goal of "resolving" the issue. Last month, that funding was approved by the Republican-controlled House Appropriations Committee, confirming that the effort to secure fair treatment for Puerto Rico is not, and should never become, a partisan issue.

The Appropriations Committee endorsed a condition proposed by the Administration, stating that federal funding will not be obligated until the Department of Justice has certified that the ballot and voter education materials are compatible with U.S. law and policy. This language was included for the specific purpose of ensuring that any PDP effort to include "New Commonwealth" as an option will not succeed. True self-determination is a choice among options that can be implemented, not an exercise in wishful thinking.

Moreover, the wording of the appropriation is key. The only way to "resolve" the island's ultimate status is through statehood or nationhood. Puerto Rico cannot resolve its status by maintaining the same undemocratic status that my people have endured since 1898 and that they rejected in November. Since the current status is the root cause of Puerto Rico's political and economic problems, it cannot also be the solution to those problems.

If the appropriation is enacted into law, I believe the leaders of this Committee can play a role in ensuring that any vote conducted pursuant to the appropriation is structured in a way that is designed to accomplish Congress's stated purpose in making the appropriation, which is to resolve the status issue once and for all.

On another front, I have introduced standalone legislation, H.R. 2000, which proceeds from the indisputable premise that statehood obtained more votes than any other option in the November referendum. The bill outlines the rights and responsibilities of statehood, and asks voters in Puerto Rico whether they accept those terms. Those who support statehood and those who oppose it—for whatever reason—will have equal opportunity to express their views. If there is a majority vote for statehood, the bill provides for the President to submit legislation to admit Puerto Rico as a State after a transition period. As of this writing, the bill enjoys support from 102 representatives from both parties and every region of the country, and it is my hope that a senator will introduce a companion bill.

In closing, I want to make this point. In June, I testified before the United Nations. I expressed faith that the U.S government would follow through on its legal and moral obligation to facilitate Puerto Rico's transition to a democratic and dignified status, but I also noted that my faith was not blind. As the leader of a party that wants Puerto Rico to become a full and equal member of the American family, I have no desire to publicly criticize the United States. But as I told the U.N., and as I reiterate now, it is more important for me to secure justice for my people than it is for me to be polite.

On November 6th, Puerto Rico withdrew its consent to territory status and expressed a preference for statehood. Congress must respect—and provide a constructive response to—the democratically expressed aspirations of its citizens.

The CHAIRMAN. Thank you very much, Commissioner.

Let's now go to Senator Berrios. Welcome.

STATEMENT OF HON. RUBÉN BERRÍOS MARTÍNEZ, PRESIDENT, THE PUERTO RICAN INDEPENDENCE PARTY

Mr. BERRIOS. Mr. Chairman, members of the committee, in 1990 the late Senator Patrick Moynihan introduced in the Congressional record an article of mine published in the Washington Post. The article warned that under territorial status Puerto Rico would inevitably become either a Commonwealth ghetto or a ghetto State. We're almost there.

Puerto Rico is [speaking Spanish.] Whereas under statehood Puerto Rico will become a ghetto State.

Last November 78 percent of eligible voters participated in a plebiscite on the political status in Puerto Rico. Two questions were posed.

The first asked voters whether or not they supported the present territorial status. 54 percent voted no, a solid and undisputable majority.

The second question asked whether they preferred independent statehood or sovereign free associated State. The result of the second question was neither clear nor irrefutable. Statehood obtained 45 percent of ballots casted and 25 percent in reference to a second question were cast blank.

Subsequently President Obama proposed a 2.5 million appropriation bill for a new status which could include the already rejected territorial status. Under the guise of inclusiveness the President of the United States has proposed political subordination as an alternative future status, the same as Senator Murkowski. This is as absurd as offering involuntary servitude or jobs below the minimum wage as remedies for unemployment.

International law demands respect for the right of self determination and Congress is empowered by the Constitution to dispose of the territory. But international law and Constitutional law, notwithstanding, Congress will not approve a plebiscite that includes a statehood option for that would be tantamount to an indirect statehood offer. A statehood offer is the death mark of any federally approved plebiscite simply because Puerto Rico's statehood is contrary to U.S. national interest.

Before last year's plebiscite the U.S. consistently argued that Puerto Rico had consented to colonial rule. Since then maintaining territorial rule always undemocratic has mutated into despotism. But the U.S. will only act to decolonize Puerto Rico when it has no other alternative.

It is therefore up to us Puerto Ricans to create a political crisis that will compel you to act.

If the statehood forces win the next election they will most probably legislate a statehood yes or no referendum.

In another scenario the present Commonwealth government could convene a Constitutional convention to negotiate a non-territorial alternative to the present status.

Inevitably, in any case, Congress will soon have to face its responsibility and make real self determination possible. Such self determination demands an informed choice between our inalienable right to independence as a distinct and separate nationality and the terms and conditions of any other non territorial alternative which the U.S. is willing to consider.

As to those terms and conditions you should recall the words of the late Patrick Moynihan on the Senate Floor in May 1990. I quote. "In the end the great issues here presented are civic, not economic. Do Puerto Ricans want to become Americans? Because that is what statehood inevitably means. Or do they wish to preserve a separate identity." I end quote.

Moreover, you must ask yourselves whether you wish the U.S. to continue as a unitary Federal State, E pluribus Unum or rather become a multinational State ruled by the motto E pluribus duo.

To conclude I bring your attention to the case of Oscar Lopez Rivera, a Puerto Rican political prisoner who has languished in U.S. prisons for more than 32 years, 32 years, longer than Nelson Mandela. Puerto Ricans, of all political persuasions, have demanded his liberation including the 3 party Presidents present here today. Surely a Nation that prides itself as a champion of human rights should take the executive decision to liberate Oscar Lopez Rivera. Justice and a sense of decency demand it.

I hope that none present over here doesn't mean that he cares so little about Puerto Rico that he's not even willing to consider making an appearance here through one of your agencies or liberate Oscar Lopez Rivera. The 3 of us demand such liberation.

[The prepared statement of Mr. Berríos Martínez follows:]

PREPARED STATEMENT OF HON. RUBÉN BERRÍOS MARTÍNEZ, PRESIDENT, THE PUERTO RICAN INDEPENDENCE PARTY

A quarter of a century ago, when the Senate was considering Puerto Rico's status issue, the late Senator Patrick D. Moynihan introduced a Washington Post article of mine in the congressional record. The article warned that, without independence, Puerto Rico would inevitably become either a commonwealth ghetto or a ghetto state.[1]

Today, with the history of the last two decades as evidence, I can sadly state that we are almost there. Puerto Rico is rapidly becoming a commonwealth ghetto; whereas under statehood Puerto Rico would become a ghetto state.

In 1990 the warning went unheeded. In 2013 Puerto Rico's unresolved status can no longer be postponed. If no action is taken, territorial status will persist. The economy, already in permanent recession, will collapse. Drug related activities and social decomposition will continue to grow, as will Puerto Rican migration to the U.S.—particularly that of our middle class and professionals. Territorial status is spent.[2]

Faced with this reality, many in Puerto Rico believe that statehood could reverse such a tendency. But a recently published article regarding the Mississippi Delta region should dispel any such illusion.[3] Although the region, embedded in 3 states, is represented in Congress by 6 senators and several congressmen corresponding to the three states in question, market laws and the economic straightjacket of the commerce clause of the U.S. constitution have turned the Mississippi Delta into a permanently depressed and marginalized zone—a regional ghetto.

---

[1] The Spanish version appears in, PUERTO RICO: NACIONALIDAD Y PLEBISCITO (1991, Editorial Libertad), p. 87-94, specifically p. 94. In 1982, in a conference in the Woodrow Wilson Center, I had already warned of that danger. See RAZON Y LUCHA (1983, Editorial Línea), p. 450.

[2] I have extensively elaborated on this matter in two Foreign Affairs articles; See "Independence for Puerto Rico, the Only Solution" (1977); and "The Decolonization of Puerto Rico" (1997).

[3] See, The Economist (June 8-14, 2013), p 33-34: "Since 1940 the region's population has fallen by almost half". . . Farm jobs have also disappeared for the most part. . . Local factories have been closing. . . Average income is just over $10,000, half the level of Mississippi as a whole and 40% of the population lives below the poverty line. The unemployment rate is 17% more than twice the national rate".

Last November, a plebiscite on political status was held in Puerto Rico. Seventy eight percent (78%) of eligible voters participated. Two questions appeared on the ballot.

The first question asked voters whether or not they agreed to maintain the present territorial relationship with the United States. A solid and indisputable majority of 54% rejected the current territorial relationship.

In the second question, voters were asked to express a preference for Independence, Statehood, or Sovereign Free Associated State. However, the result of the second question was neither clear nor irrefutable. Statehood obtained 45% of all ballots cast. There were approximately 25% blank ballots on the second question; and only by factoring those ballots out—which were definitely not in favor of statehood—can it be argued that statehood obtained 61% of the vote.[4]

Subsequently, President Obama submitted a budget proposal of $2.5 million dollars for "voters education," if the Puerto Rican government legislated another status vote. Furthermore, the President openly invited the Puerto Rican government to include the resoundingly rejected territorial status among the options. Under the guise of inclusiveness, the President has proposed political subordination as an alternative future status. Such a recommendation is no more justifiable and no less absurd and undemocratic than offering jobs below the minimum wage or involuntary servitude as remedies for unemployment.

Congress, empowered by the Constitution to dispose of the territory, has yet to act. Moreover, International law has recognized the right of all peoples to self-determination which, under treaty obligations assumed by the United States, is part of U.S. law. Thus the U.S. could, ideally, fulfill its obligations under U.N. Res 1514 (XV). However, it could also ignore international law and pass legislation for a federally sponsored plebiscite among non-territorial options.

I am well aware, however, that international and constitutional law notwithstanding, Congress will not approve a plebiscite which includes a statehood option. The reason is simple. To offer such an option would tantamount to an indirect statehood offer, were that option to prevail in a plebiscite. A statehood option is the death mark of any federally sponsored plebiscite simply because Puerto Rican statehood is contrary to U.S. national interests.

You should, therefore, speak frankly and tell Puerto Ricans which alternatives you will consider to comply with your decolonization obligation. But unfortunately, at this stage, you are not willing to frankly discard statehood as an alternative for fear of seeming racist or undemocratic.

Consequently, no status legislation will be approved by Congress. U.S. policy therefore remains undemocratically clear: to perpetuate a territorial status which the majority of Puerto Ricans repudiate.

In the end, however, you will not be able to avoid the difficult decisions regarding Puerto Rico's unresolved status. U.S. policy promoting dependence under the existing territorial status, coupled with a long history of anti-independence repression, has inevitably led many of our compatriots to think that two senators and six representatives would suffice to ensure an eternal cornucopia of federal funds.

Time is running out. Before last November's plebiscite, the US government consistently argued that Puerto Rico had consented to colonial rule. Since then, territorial rule—always undemocratic—has mutated into despotism.

We are well aware, that the U.S. Government will act to decolonize Puerto Rico only when it has no other alternative. It is therefore up to us, in Puerto Rico, to create a political crisis that will force you to act.

Different scenarios are possible. The statehood forces may win the 2016 elections and enact legislation calling for a "Statehood Yes or No" referendum, similar to the one they are now proposing, and try to secure a majority vote for statehood.

Another possible scenario is that the present Commonwealth government would muster the necessary political will to convene a Status Convention to negotiate a non-colonial alternative to the present status.

The Puerto Rican people have rejected the territorial relation. Inevitably, Congress will have to make true self-determination possible. Self-determination demands that the U.S. spell out a fair and equitable transition so that the Puerto

---

[4] As a matter of law, Puerto Rico's Electoral Code requires that blank votes be counted. The Supreme Court of Puerto Rico has recognized since 1993 "the right [of a voter] to deposit his blank ballot in the ballot box, as a means to express that he or she does not a favor any of the proposed status options". Sánchez y Colón v. ELA, 134 DPR 445 (1993); and 134 DPR 503 (1993). More recently, in 2009, the Supreme Court of Puerto Rico ruled that, "[w]e may reasonably conclude that the voter who voluntarily. . . deposits his blank ballot. . .had the clear intention not to favor any of the options. . .on the ballot". Suárez Cáceres v. CEE, 176 DPR 31 (2009).

Rican people can exercise an informed choice between independence, which is our inalienable right as a distinct and separate nationality, and the terms and conditions of any other non-territorial alternative the U.S. is willing to consider.

That time will come soon. And when it does, it would be wise to recall the words of the late senator Patrick D. Moynihan (D-NY) on the Senate floor in May 1990: "In the end, the great issues presented here are civic, not economic. Do Puerto Ricans wish to become Americans? Because that is what statehood ineluctably implies. Or do they wish to preserve a separate identity?"[5]

You should then frankly tell the Puerto Rican people that to become a state they must be willing to become Americans and renounce their identity as a separate and distinct nationality. You must also ask yourselves, whether you wish the U.S. to continue as a unitary federal state under the guiding maxim of E pluribus unum; or whether you want your country to become a multinational state ruled instead by the motto of E pluribus duo.[6]

Since actions speak louder than words, I want to conclude by bringing to your attention the case of Oscar López Rivera, a Puerto Rican political prisoner who has languished in U.S. prisons for more than 32 years—longer than Nelson Mandela. Puerto Ricans of all political persuasions have demanded his liberation, including the three party presidents present here today. Surely a nation that prides itself as champion of human rights should, through executive action, liberate Oscar López Rivera.

Justice and a sense of decency demand it.

The CHAIRMAN. Thanks. Thank you all for eloquent presentations.

Let me just ask a few questions. I'm going to, in effect, ask them to the panel and then I know my colleagues are anxious to ask questions as well.

In November, a majority of voters opposed continuation of the current territory status. Looking forward to the plebiscite proposed by the President, do you, and we can just go down the row, believe that the Election Commission should agree that the current territory status should not be on the ballot?

Let us just go right down the row. We start with you, Governor. Each one of you if you can answer yes or no that would be helpful.

Mr. PADILLA. OK.

Thank you, Chairman.

First, Commonwealth wasn't there. Commonwealths cannot be defined as governed territorial statute. That's a mistake because we called the Commonwealth a territory is a question of law.

Being a question of law I want to state in this committee a word of a sitting judge of the United States of America, Mr. Justice Breyer when he was in the first Circuit Court. The case is Caldav versus Chase. I quote. "In sum Puerto Rico's status change from that of mere territory——

The CHAIRMAN. Governor, I want to be respectful. But my time is going to go by very quickly. I have other questions.

Do you believe that the Election Commission should agree that the current territory status should not be on the ballot?

Mr. PADILLA. It's a mistake to call Commonwealth governed territorial status. The Commonwealth wasn't there. The Commonwealth wasn't it.

Imagine, Senator, and that's why it's only a paragraph.

---

[5] See also, Letter by President-Elect Bill Clinton, to Governor-Elect of Puerto Rico, Pedro J. Rosselló, December 30, 1992, recognizing "the distinct identity which Puerto Ricans have developed since the first encounter with Hispanic culture and the Island."

[6] For a more elaborate discussion of this issue, see my statement before the Senate Energy and Natural Resources Committee, January 30, 1991.

When the Federal Government relation with Puerto Rico changed from being bounded merely by the Territory Act laws and the right of the people of Puerto Rico as United States citizens to being bounded, listen carefully, to being bounded by the United States and Puerto Rico Constitution. Public loss in hundreds, 600. Puerto Rico Federation Act and the rights of the people of Puerto Rico as U.S. citizens.

I cannot call the United States of America the Empire of the West because it is a mistake.

I cannot place in a ballot Commonwealth independence and Federal taxes and losing Olympic Committee and losing our national identity because that does the name of statehood. Commonwealth have and needs to be——

The CHAIRMAN. Governor, again, my time is going to run out even before we get through one question.

I think what you're telling me is you want another option on the ballot.

Mr. PADILLA. No, commonwealth needs to be there and as Felix Frankfurter says, address the issue of a non-State jurisdiction of the interstate is an issue of statesmanship, creative statesmanship.

The CHAIRMAN. But we're just going to have to move on.

Let's see, let's now go to the Commissioner.

Commissioner, do you believe that the Election Commission should agree that the current territory status should not be on the ballot?

Mr. PIERLUISI. I take it you're basing the question on the pending appropriation request from the President which calls for a process to, I quote. "Solve Puerto Rico status."

You cannot solve the problem of our status by including the very option that was rejected by our people. Elections, as well as plebiscites, have consequences. The people were asked very simply, do you want Puerto Rico to continue having its current status?

They said, resoundingly, no.

So the options should be statehood, free association and independence. The 3 alternatives we have to the current status.

The CHAIRMAN. Senator, same question.

Do you believe the Election Commission should agree that the current territory status should not be on the ballot?

Mr. BERRIOS. Of course not.

First because——

The CHAIRMAN. You said no. Oh my goodness. I got an answer. [Laughter.]

The CHAIRMAN. Thank you.

Mr. BERRIOS. I'm very straight forward.

The CHAIRMAN. You are indeed.

Mr. BERRIOS. I'm for independence.

The CHAIRMAN. Thank you. Very good.

Alright.

I am a little curious. I would like to be respectful; would you like to amplify on your no answer?

Mr. BERRIOS. No. We already said no. To ask us again would be as absurd as asking to accept involuntary servitude already rejected by Puerto Rican people, it's absurd.

The CHAIRMAN. Alright.

Let me see if I can get one other question in with respect to translating this issue of free association.

One of the choices on the November ballot was sovereign free association. In English, this phrase would be taken to mean the current free association relationship between the U.S. and the 3 nations of the former U.S. administered trust territory of the Pacific.

However, some are concerned that when this phrase is expressed in Spanish voters may confuse it with the Spanish phrase for the current Commonwealth or the proposed enhanced Commonwealth.

So my question here is for each of you gentlemen. Do you think that this concern about confusion through translation is a valid one?

Mr. PADILLA. Yes.

The CHAIRMAN. Very good.

[Laughter.]

The CHAIRMAN. Your colleagues.

Mr. PIERLUISI. No, I do not believe that that creates much confusion. In Puerto Rico our voters are well educated about the options we have.

The CHAIRMAN. Senator.

Mr. PIERLUISI. We have debated this topic long enough.

The CHAIRMAN. Very good.

Mr. BERRIOS. That phrase was invented by Puerto Rican colonists in 1952. They call it Commonwealth here so in the past as a Commonwealth of Pennsylvania or Massachusetts. They call it free associated State there in order to confuse the people thinking it was some sort of a sovereign association.

But now, 60 years later.

The CHAIRMAN. You think——

Mr. BERRIOS. Obviously no one is going to be confused by that.

The CHAIRMAN. So people are not going to be confused in your view?

Mr. BERRIOS. Of course not.

The CHAIRMAN. Very good.

Senator Murkowski.

Senator MURKOWSKI. Since we're talking about definitions here and whether or not they cause some confusion.

Governor, can you define exactly what enhanced Commonwealth really means because I'm not sure that I understand it.

Mr. PADILLA. Thank you, Senator, for that question. It is a very valid one.

A good example of serious consideration by Congress of the enhanced development of Commonwealth may be found in the legislative process between 1989 and 1991 and during the 1975 ad hoc procedure.

But in 1975 a young fellow of the Department of Justice quote in a letter. "The proposed compact would without altering the fundamental nature of Puerto Rico's Commonwealth status provides substantially increased autonomy to the island's government and its people."

We can talk about for example, that those processes that have been already studied by Congress and by the Commonwealths to see what's last parallels apply to Puerto Rico that cannot damage the possibility of economic development of Puerto Rico or the language in further, in courts in Puerto Rico that should be Spanish. That young fellow, the name of that young fellow back in 1975, Mitchell McConnell, Jr., Minority Leader in the Senate.

Senator MURKOWSKI. Governor, what I'm trying to understand is exactly what enhanced Commonwealth is and the question really here is whether or not it's consistent with the U.S. Constitution.

Now I understand that your legislature has passed this resolution that, when we're talking about the plebiscite it says, incorporates all options including the enhanced Commonwealth. But if our Department of Justice should determine that enhanced Commonwealth does not, in fact, meet with the definitions within our U.S. Constitution, doesn't fit within that. We've got a situation here where you're going to have a plebiscite that, again, is not going to be followed or upheld.

So what I'm trying to understand is how we're defining this and is it consistent with our Constitution.

Mr. PADILLA. Again——

Senator MURKOWSKI. Because we recognize that there is a challenge there.

Mr. PADILLA. Again, great question.

But is something that all of us know. Whoever write the Constitution—of something is the Supreme Court. The Supreme Court already resolve this issue.

Let's see U.S. versus Latta, the same judge, Mr. Justice Breyer.

Third, Congress statutory goal to modify the degree of our autonomy and joy by the dependent sovereigning that is not a State, is not unusual the—objective. The political branches drawing upon another one's Constitutional authority. Authority have made adjusting to the autonomous statutes of other such dependent entities sometimes making far more radical adjustments than those at issue here.

That the Supreme Court decision, you can, of course it's Constitutional. The Supreme Court has stated that every time that have been asked.

Senator MURKOWSKI. I would suggest that there is still an issue there in terms of the Constitutionality. This is part of what we're dealing with in trying to understand here.

Let me ask you a question here, Commissioner Pierluisi.

I mentioned in my opening statement that when Alaska was seeking statehood it was Alaskans engaged, very, very engaged in pushing toward statehood. In fact, at the time that the case was successfully made it was about over 80 percent of the Alaskan electorate supported that, an overwhelming majority.

Do you think that Congress should consider a statehood petition if the status does not have a majority, let alone a super majority of the voters?

Mr. PIERLUISI. Let me answer this way.

We are driving the process the same way Alaska did back in the 1950s. Different times, though. This is the 21st century. But we're driving the process.

We just held a vote in Puerto Rico. As I said, plebiscites, as elections, have consequences. The people rejected the current status.

This is the most Democratic Nation in the world and you cannot ignore that vote. You need to respond to that vote.

One way of responding is the way that I am proposing in the House, H.R. 2000. It calls, it basically lays out statehood for the voters of Puerto Rico and asks for an up or down vote on the admission of Puerto Rico as a State. Then provides the steps that the Federal Government would take to admit Puerto Rico as a State if that's the wish of the majority of the people of Puerto Rico.

But that's driven by Puerto Rico because I represent Puerto Rico in Congress.

Now, by the way, you asked the question. If you allow me, let me quickly answer. What the PDP has been proposing for a long time now is that the relationship between Puerto Rico and the U.S. be based on a compact or treaty that cannot be changed by either party, must be changed by mutual agreement. That, in and of itself, is unconstitutional.

In addition, what you're proposing is that Puerto Rico would keep the same level of Federal funding, yet have the ability to decide with Federal laws apply in Puerto Rico and which do not. I am sure that many colleagues representing the states would like to have that power as well.

That's why consistently, among other reasons the Federal Government, the OJ, as well as this committee and the counterpart committee in the House have said that such proposal isn't Constitutional. It violates public policy. The name doesn't change the nature of the status.

Puerto Rico is, as a matter of law, an unincorporated territory of the United States. It is called a Commonwealth because the Constitution of Puerto Rico which was approved by the U.S. Congress, calls the government of Puerto Rico the Commonwealth of Puerto Rico. I try to be brief, but I believe that answers your question.

They're proposing unconstitutional, an unconstitutional relationship with the U.S. That's why it cannot be on the ballot. But the current status, call it as you may, Commonwealth, unincorporated territory, Puerto Rico, call it whatever. It was rejected by the people of Puerto Rico.

We've waited long enough. We want Congress to take action.

Senator MURKOWSKI. Mr. Chairman, my time is expired.

The CHAIRMAN. Senator Heinrich.

Senator HEINRICH. Thank you, Mr. Chairman.

I want to ask Governor Garcia Padilla, under what you're calling an enhanced Commonwealth would Puerto Rico be subject to all the Federal laws that the Congress, House and Senate, signed by the President are passed or would you pick and choose which laws under——

Mr. PADILLA. No, no one is trying to mislead you. If anyone tell you that we want to pick. What had been studied in 1975 process, with approval of the Department of Justice, but what state to Congress in 1989 to 1991 process and passed the House unanimously was the process between Congress and Puerto Rico. Both will agree if there's any Federal law that can damage in a different way without damaging the effect of that law in the states, damage the possibility of the economy of Puerto Rico to move on. So it's the process between the Congress and the people of Puerto Rico, not a picking process.

Senator HEINRICH. So, Governor, what exactly is an enhanced Commonwealth?

Mr. PADILLA. Let's go for example. It has been studied very well. As I told you it passed the House already once in the state here, in the Senate.

We can arrange that way where Federal laws which apply to Puerto Rico, but in a mutual, working together, with Congress not Puerto Rico alone.

We can talk about Federal courts in Puerto Rico not about the application of the Federal court to Puerto Rico, but the language there. The Federal courts in Puerto Rico is struggling with the language in Puerto Rico because most of Puerto Ricans speak Spanish.

There you have two examples.

But let me tell you something, Senator. To take Commonwealth out of the ballot is——

Senator HEINRICH. I think we've already established that.

Mr. PADILLA. But I didn't answer that.

Senator HEINRICH. There's a very clear question on the ballot in November. People made a decision. I think we have to respect that decision.

Mr. PADILLA. I know, but the Commonwealth wasn't there.

Senator HEINRICH. Is there——

Mr. PADILLA. That's a disenfranchisement.

Senator HEINRICH. I would submit that there are 4 constitutionally valid options here, the Commonwealth, independence, statehood and free association.

Mr. PADILLA. I agree.

Senator HEINRICH. In my reading of this ballot it's fairly clear that the voters rejected Commonwealth status.

Mr. PADILLA. Commonwealth was there?

Senator HEINRICH. That gives us 3 remaining choices. I think, you know, we sort of danced semantically around this for long enough that we have to move forward and begin to make some decisions here.

I want to move on to Commissioner Pierluisi.

you introduced a bill in the House, I understand, that would just hold a straight up or down vote on statehood. If what people are saying about the intent of voters who left their ballots blank that's a fairly risky proposition. But obviously you believe that that's the best way to get a very clear idea of how people feel on statehood.

Say that vote comes out favorably to what you want to see and the voters in Puerto Rico vote yes. Walk us through the next steps because obviously that doesn't result immediately in statehood, of all the steps we'd have to walk through to actually see that come to fruition and see Puerto Rico become a State.

Mr. PIERLUISI. The bill provides that the President shall submit an admission bill admitting Puerto Rico as a State within the period of 180 days. The bill should include a transition period during which additional Federal moneys would flow into Puerto Rico and Federal contributions would be gradually applied.

The Congress, the bill, then provides that Congress is committed to act on the legislation and so and admit Puerto Rico.

The bill, as it says in its first sentence, sets forth the process for admitting Puerto Rico as a State of the Union. So it is an admission bill. It provides that process that I just laid out for you.

Senator HEINRICH. OK.

Thank you, Chairman.

The CHAIRMAN. Thank you very much.

Mr. BERRIOS. Mr. Chairman.

The CHAIRMAN. Yes, indeed.

Mr. BERRIOS. I would like to add a couple of points.

The CHAIRMAN. Please.

Mr. BERRIOS. They've had plenty of time.

The CHAIRMAN. Please.

Mr. BERRIOS. Mr. Chairman, nobody knows what enhanced Commonwealth means. They've been trying to define it for half a century. Nobody knows. So the answer is nobody knows.

This is just political hocus pocus, political bull, to put it in plain English. So you shouldn't stress the point anymore because they won't define it. In definition it is their name for the territory. The territory has been repudiated by 54 percent of the Puerto Rican people. Now it has to—itself into tyranny.

So it seems to me here since you want information to take positive steps ahead. We're in the middle of a discussion similar to those held in the Middle Ages where people ask how many angels fit into a needles head.

You won't approve anything that says, even indirectly, you will accept statehood. So as long as statehood is in his bill or your bill, nothing will happen. As long as Commonwealth remains, we remain a colony, a territory. It's about time you start speaking frankly to the Puerto Rican people. Telling them what are the conditions under which you would accept, if you could accept statehood. Refuse to consider colonialism any longer and make a reasonable offer between our inalienable right to govern ourselves either under independence or any other formula of a non territorial relation.

If it's statehood, state the conditions for statehood.

If it's free association, state the conditions of free association.

That's the way to go. If not, we're losing our time once more in this, the Senate's time and our time.

The CHAIRMAN. Recognizing the perils of asking for a yes or no answer.

[Laughter.]

The CHAIRMAN. I'm going to try once more on an issue that I do think there is some common ground. I hope that there is.

Governor, we'll start with you.

Should the ballot question under the President's proposal be simplified to statehood, yes or no or sovereignty, yes or no?

Mr. PADILLA. No. I want to tell you why.

First, take commonwealth out of the ballot is a way to disenfranchise the majority of the people of Puerto Rico that have vote for the Commonwealth every time the Commonwealth has been in the ballot. This time the Commonwealth wasn't there.

Second, I'm not for independence, as you know. But I have to protect the right of the pro-independence people to have their option on the ballot.

Mr. BERRIOS. Thank you.

Mr. PADILLA. You're welcome.

[Laughter.]

Mr. PADILLA. I'm not pro-statehood that will make Puerto Rico a Latino ghetto. I have to defend pro-statehooders to have their option on the ballot.

I cannot disenfranchise them. It's not pay back time for me because I want to disenfranchise in November. What the pro-statehood party is asking you, Chairman and this committee, is to be accomplish of that Democratic crime, crime against democracy.

Take the one who won. Always the people have been ask out of the ballot because if the Commonwealth is in the ballot, they have no way to win.

The CHAIRMAN. Governor, the reason that I asked the question was leaders in your party have endorsed statehood, yes or no, for this committee in 2010 and in hearings before the House Resources Committee in 2009. That's why it's relevant.

Let me get——

Mr. PADILLA. Let me add something.

The CHAIRMAN. Let me get your colleagues——

Mr. PADILLA. Let me add something, Senator.

People in pro-statehood party have expressed that they are not agree with the yes or no for statehood process. So that's a democracy.

The CHAIRMAN. What your leaders in the past endorsed was framing the issue around statehood, yes or no. That's a matter of public record.

So let me just get your colleagues into this. And let me have the other Senators ask any remaining questions.

Mr. PIERLUISI. I'll be brief.

By definition when you pose a question that's a yes or no question you're not excluding anybody because whoever is in support of the proposition can vote yes. Whoever is against can vote no. So, to talk about excluding anybody when you're posing an up or down question, it's just nonsensical.

Now whether we can use the $2.5 million for consulting the people of Puerto Rico on the admission of Puerto Rico, potential admission of Puerto Rico, as a State, of course, we can. It is consistent with the language of the appropriation because it is directed to resolving the issue of Puerto Rico status and definitely one of the options through which you can solve this problem is by admitting Puerto Rico as a State.

The other option I do not support because there's no support for, majority support. You cannot even argue there's anything close to it for Puerto Rico becoming a national—treated as a sovereign Nation.

But again, I would say that if somebody proposes that vote what's going to happen is that the overwhelming majority of Puerto Ricans will vote against. So I wouldn't say that I'm being excluded as a state-hooder. I would simply vote no if the question is the second one that you post.

The CHAIRMAN. Senator.

Mr. BERRIOS. If statehood yes or no——

The CHAIRMAN. Or sovereignty, yes or no.

Mr. BERRIOS. Statehood first. If statehood yes or no referendum stemming from this Congress is an impossible proposition. You will never get it passed through even this committee. I can assure you that through 30 years of experience.

The United States will never make such an offer. So that's out of the question.

Now, regarding the second question.

We have an inalienable right to independence under international law. If you are willing to make statement publicly and push through a status referendum where you offer independence with a reasonable transition, as it should be for your benefit and for our benefit, of course I would accept independence, independence yes or no referendum.

The CHAIRMAN. Let's do this.

I'm going to let my colleagues ask any additional questions and then give my assessment of where we are at this point. I will tell you I thought it was particularly noteworthy giving some of the history of Senator Murkowski. In fact, the current Senator Murkowski knows a little bit about this because in 2001 the U.S. Department of Justice wrote to the former Chairman of this committee, who was Senator Murkowski's father, Frank Murkowski, with the finding that enhanced Commonwealth is inconsistent with the Constitution.

So this debate has been running a little while.

Senator MURKOWSKI. A long while.

The CHAIRMAN. Senator Murkowski, the current Senator Murkowski.

Senator MURKOWSKI. Let me ask you a question, Senator Berrios, because you brought up the issue of self determination.

Mr. BERRIOS. Yes.

Senator MURKOWSKI. The right of all peoples to self determination. But then in response to another colleague here, you indicated that look, we here in Congress should just set out these conditions.

You've said territorial status is out. It should be dropped.

That the option for statehood is unrealistic.

But if we were to basically provide these conditions to you, isn't that just another form of Washington, DC, dictating to Puerto Rico whether it's the level of status or the conditions. How does that address this right of self determination that you've spoken of?

Mr. BERRIOS. Senator Murkowski, when you came into Puerto Rico in 1998 you asked nobody. You just invaded. I don't mean you. You were a territory.

Senator MURKOWSKI. Thank you.

Mr. BERRIOS. The United States invaded Puerto Rico and consulted nobody. Under the law, international law you should devolve our powers so we can exercise our free determination. That is not going to happen, of course.

You would only do that when you have no other option.

We accept that statehood be put in a plebiscite in the future after the United—if it's through a congressional—if the United States is willing to spell out the conditions for statehood.

Senator MURKOWSKI. You don't think that that's them dictating in violation of your right to self determination?

Mr. BERRIOS. No, no, no. No because the only right you have as a Nation, as a Nation, not as Alaskans, not as Hawaiians, nor as Texas, as a Nation, the only right is the right to independence juridically.

We know we are not the majority in Puerto Rico. What we say is that if a referendum was going to be held through an act of Congress, independence has to be included with a transitional period which should be included independence. If any other options is going to be included through an act of Congress, free association or statehood, then you should spell out whether you are willing to grant that, once it is approved because once independence wins a referendum there's an option.

You have to act upon a petition for independence. We're in the 21st century, not in 1898. That's what I mean.

Senator MURKOWSKI. Mr.——

Mr. PIERLUISI. Could I comment?

Senator MURKOWSKI. Commissioner, go ahead.

Mr. PIERLUISI. I want to try to be brief.

The same way you cannot impose statehood on Puerto Rico, we, the American citizens of Puerto Rico, cannot impose statehood on you. Definitely you can lay out the terms and conditions for statehood. But by the way, we're not seeking a special statehood for Puerto Rico. It would be statehood on equal footing with the 50 other States.

The only terms and conditions you would be laying out would be, for example, the transition period because this doesn't have to happen overnight. You can provide for a 6 year transition period, 8-year transition period, in which you would gradually give us parity. We don't have parity, equal treatment in Federal programs.

At the same time you would gradually impose Federal taxes on the island, income taxes. So that's the only aspect that under which we could have a different treatment than the states. It would only last during the transition period.

But, of course, you're not, it's like for a change of status to happen two things must happen.

Congress must provide for it.

The people of Puerto Rico must accept it.

So you cannot detract yourself from the process. You have to be engaged. We're driving the process in the sense that we already held a plebiscite. We can, very much so, morally and legally do it. We're telling you, act on it. Respond to it.

Mr. BERRIOS. Senator, if you permit me for a moment?

Senator MURKOWSKI. Senator.

Mr. BERRIOS. There's one condition for statehood which the Resident Commissioner hasn't mentioned. It's Senator Moynihan's questions.

Do Puerto Ricans know they have to become Americans in order to become a State of the Union or do they want their own separate identity? That's the undemocratic transition. It deals with the way of being, the Nation of being Puerto Rican. That's called a nationality under international law.

We are a distinct nationality. Do we want to continue as a distinct nationality? Congress should be clear like Senator Moynihan who was an expert on these matters.

You want to become a State of the Union you have to become Americans. You cannot maintain your separate identity in the long run. That's a condition also which should be spelled out.

The CHAIRMAN. Senator Heinrich.

Senator HEINRICH. Senator Berrios, following up on that idea what would you think of a ballot that first asks up front, you know, should Puerto Rico be part of the United States?

Yes or no?

If the answer is yes than you choose on the second tier between statehood and the current status, Commonwealth status.

Mr. BERRIOS. Of course not because you cannot exclude independence in any valid plebiscite.

Senator HEINRICH. But if they say no.

Mr. BERRIOS. No, but you can——

Senator HEINRICH. You go and choose independence and free association.

Mr. BERRIOS. It's been part of the United States does not include independence. Independence means independence.

Senator HEINRICH. Right, no, I know. I recognize that.

I agree with you. But if so, if the people of Puerto Rico vote no, we should not be part of the United States then——

Mr. BERRIOS. No, no. It's not being part of the United States. It's independence. It's as positive as—like the United States. You are independent. You have a right as a Nation to be independent.

We are a colony of the United States. What you can ask us is whether we want to become independent or not, that you can ask, not whether we want to be part of the United States.

Of course we don't want to be part of the United States as a colony. The Federalists don't want it. Neither do we want it.

Senator HEINRICH. Commissioner, do you have an opinion on that?

Mr. PIERLUISI. My reaction is that if you pose a question like that probably 80 to 90 percent of the people will say that they want Puerto Rico to continue to be part of the United States actually. Legally, if we go by the Supreme Court precedent, it's not technically part. It's just——

Mr. BERRIOS. Belongs to.

Mr. PIERLUISI. It belongs to. It is possession or a territory of the United States. But the answer would be overwhelming. The same way, as I said before, if you pose a question national sovereignty, yes or no?

I'm telling you the overwhelming majority are going to vote against national sovereignty.

To react to something that Senator Berrios just told you. We are proud American citizens. I know, I respect my fellow independent from Puerto Rico. I do respect them and their ideal.

But you know, we're proud American citizens. If you poll in Puerto Rico whether people want to continue having their American citizenship, it's going to be like 80 or 90 percent again. So the votes should be meaningful.

That question to me is not meaningful because we already know the answer to it.

Mr. BERRIOS. Senator, of course we respect independent people. Everybody in the world does, you know.

[Laughter.]

Mr. BERRIOS [continuing]. Or Commonwealthers and I'm very glad that after 60 years of persecution of independent forces now we have the right to speak, like, you know.

This is all—we could blabber on for—nothing is going to happen here. Nothing. You will not act. I repeat.

Do not fool yourself. You will not act as long as there is a possibility offered. You will not act. But you have to act to decolonize.

Think about it. How do you do it? How do you decolonize without including statehood as one of the alternatives.

Senator, Pierluisi said, Resident Commissioner's bill will go nowhere. This means I am grateful that it will go nowhere.

Senator HEINRICH. Governor, you wanted to add something?

Mr. PADILLA. Yes, Senator, thank you.

Precisely on the White House Task Force report they suggest the idea of a two question referendum on if we want to remain part of the United States, be in the Commonwealth and statehood, the alternative and not independence of sovereign being not part. The two options that win will go to a second question. We endorse that.

But let me go farther. To exclude—let's say for the sake of argument that Commonwealth and what they call current territorial status the same. We have to exclude that.

Statehood lose in 1993, in 1998 in 1967. We are not proposing to exclude statehood because they lose. Exclude the Commonwealth from the ballot is disenfranchisement. That's why I am in favor of including all the formulas, all the ballot formulas, all the ballot options in the ballots. I think that's fairness.

The majority of the people of Puerto Rico have been voting for the Commonwealth every time the Commonwealth is in the ballot. Now they want to take it, disenfranchise the majority of Puerto Rico.

I know that you, Senator, not the Chairman, not the Senator Murkowski will take place and that will be taking place.

Mr. BERRIOS. Talking what?

Mr. PADILLA. Talking place on——

The CHAIRMAN. Let me give you my assessment of where we are.

First, gentlemen, you should know that this committee has made a special focus on trying to resolve issues that I usually characterize as running longer than the Trojan War. They just kind of go on and on and on. We've had some success in a number of areas.

A few weeks ago there was a report in one of the newspapers that we had sent more bills to the Floor of the U.S. Senate than all the other Committees together. So that's because we try to find common ground.

We are going to need your leadership here in order to do that.

Let me give you my take in terms of where we are.

I think we made some progress.

Two out of 3 of you seem to believe that the current status and enhanced Commonwealth are no longer options. They're no longer options on the table, two out of 3 of you.

So looking forward it seems to me that it's especially important to see if the 3 of you can come to an agreement on the language of a ballot that, in effect, has 2 remaining options: statehood, or sovereignty as an independent or freely associated State.

Absent an agreement of the 3 of you it seems that this will just go round and round some more. So we very much look forward to working with you. I'm sure the people of Puerto Rico want this resolved. We are interested in working constructively and closely with you.

So unless Senator Murkowski wants to add anything else, or Senator Heinrich, I'll let Senator Murkowski have the last word.

Senator MURKOWSKI. I don't mean to have the last word.

The CHAIRMAN. No, sure.

Senator MURKOWSKI. But I wanted to share with you a thought that I just shared with the Chairman here in reflecting on Alaska's statehood fight. It was a 90-plus year fight. I'm reminded that it took us 90 years to get to statehood and for us the only decision was up or down on statehood.

The fact that Puerto Rico has been engaged in this issue for also, many, many decades, but the fact that you have as many options as you do makes it perhaps, even more difficult than Alaska faced when it was just an up or down. As I would agree with the Chairman that the process for determining what the options will be on the ballot and how they are defined, is as critical as anything that we have discussed here today.

So it's a challenge to you and those that you represent to try to address how we define what the options are and then how they would therefore be defined on this ballot moving forward.

So, I thank the Chairman. Certainly thank you, gentlemen, for leading the discussion here this morning.

The CHAIRMAN. Gentlemen, thank you.

As you can see, the Senators here and both political parties want to work closely with you and get this resolved.

With that the Energy Committee is adjourned.

[Whereupon, at 10:58 a.m. the hearing was adjourned.]

APPENDIX

ADDITIONAL MATERIAL SUBMITTED FOR THE RECORD

————————

ALIANZA PRO LIBRE ASOCIACIÓN SOBERANA,
(ALLIANCE FOR SOVEREIGN FREE ASSOCIATION),
Mayagüez, PR, July 18, 2013.

Hon. RON WYDEN,
*Chairman, Senate Committee on Energy and Natural Resources, 304 Dirksen Senate
Building, Washington, DC.*

DEAR SENATOR WYDEN:

The Committee on Energy and Natural Resources (CENR) has scheduled a Status Hearing Session to be held on August 1, 2013 "to receive testimony on the November 6, 2012 referendum [plebiscite] on the political status of Puerto Rico and the Administration's response." As publicly announced, the three political parties that participated in the plebiscite in representation of one or two of the questions to be answered during the vote were invited to depose before the CENR. To my knowledge, no other groups or organizations were invited. Unfortunately, this leaves out the Alliance for Sovereign Free Association (ALAS, by its Spanish acronym), which I am honored to represent as its acting president.

As you probably know, although not a political party ALAS is a citizens organization that was certified by the Puerto Rico Elections Commission to represent the option of Sovereign Free Associated State (Estado Libre Asociado Soberano or ELA Soberano), one of the status alternatives in the aforementioned referendum. This option obtained 454,768 votes (33.34% of total votes). Therefore, by excluding ALAS, the CENR in fact leaves these voters without a legitimately recognized voice during the Hearing.

The CENR's actions with respect to ALAS might be construed as an unintentional oversight, but many view it as disrespectful—or at the least, inconsiderate—towards the only organization that has official recognition as the defender of Free Association, an option that may very well become the status preference of the majority of Puerto Rican's, and probably the most convenient for the United States of America as well. I stress this point because future congressional actions may require the representation of the free association option and, at present, that representation falls upon ALAS. This fact should not be overlooked by the CENR if its procedures are truly to be dressed in the cloth of democracy.

Be it as it may, ALAS still wants to make its case before the CENR and, therefore, asks that this letter and the enclosed written statement be accepted by the Committee and included in the CENR's record of the Status Hearing Session. We believe this to be of sufficient importance as to merit mention during the Hearing, at least to the extent that you publicly state a reasonable and accurate synopsis of our position which, we stress once again, is the position of the 33.4% of the voters we represent.

Sincerely,

JOSÉ L. ARBONA,
ALAS, Acting President.

————————

STATEMENT OF JENNIFFER A. GONZÁLEZ-COLÓN, NEW PROGRESSIVE PARTY LEADER AND FORMER SPEAKER, PUERTO RICO HOUSE OF REPRESENTATIVES

Mr. Chairman, Ranking Minority Member Murkowski, and other Distinguished Members:

Thank you for holding this hearing on Puerto Rico's plebiscite on the territory's political status last November and the Obama Administration's response.

The territory's status is the central issue of the islands, which have a population of nearly 3.7 million. It is fundamental: whether Puerto Ricans will continue to be Americans and obtain equality within the country or become the people of a separate nation, and whether there is another alternative other than temporary, powerless, and unequal territory status. The issue defines our politics and political parties. It is a basic issue of democracy, which requires representative government—a right we lack at the national government level. It raises questions about the appropriate Federal as well as territorial policies on many issues. It retards our economic and social development.

Puerto Rico has been under the U.S. flag since the United States took the islands in connection with the Spanish-American War and Congress has granted U.S. citizenship since 1917, but Congress has not yet determined the ultimate status of the territory.

The Federal government has professed a policy of 'self-determination' for decades. But Congress has unintentionally enabled a minority in Puerto Rico to confuse and frustrate a local decision among Puerto Rico's status options. Congress has let this happen by not acting clearly and as a whole on the questions of Federal law and policy that are the primary issues raised by the alternative to statehood, nationhood, and territory status for which a minority still hopes.

The plebiscite and some presidential and congressional actions since have made important strides towards resolution of the issue—but the Obama Administration and the Congress need to do more in the interests of the Nation as well as of the territory.

According to the U.S. Supreme Court, Puerto Rico is an unincorporated territory under the broad powers of Congress to govern territories except to the extent that the fundamental rights of individuals would be infringed. Our people have been permitted to exercise self-government on local affairs similar to the authority that States possess.

But we are only represented in the government that makes our national laws by a sole resident commissioner in the House of Representatives who can only vote in committees to which she or he is assigned.

Additionally, although Puerto Rico is considered to be a State under most laws, it—and its residents—can be—and are—treated differently than the States and the District of Columbia in some major programs. The differences disadvantage most Puerto Ricans, although there are some tax benefits for companies and individuals from the States and for the wealthy.

The United States did not make clear during the first half of the last century that Puerto Rico would eventually obtain equality within the Nation. It discouraged independence. Meanwhile, Puerto Ricans grew close to the United States and prized U.S. citizenship and other benefits of being a U.S. area.

These factors resulted in some nationalists seeking to create a new political status: a hybrid of statehood, nationhood, and territory status. Proposals for such a status have been made in every decade beginning in the 1950s.

Federal Executive and/or Legislative branch officials have always seriously considered the proposals. But, ultimately, the proposals have always been rejected as conflicting with the Constitution and basic laws and policies of the United States and impossible for structure of government reasons.

The proposals are called words in Spanish that literally translate as "Associated Free State" and are referred to as "Commonwealth" in English. The names come from the names of Puerto Rico's local government adopted with the territorial constitution.

In authorizing the constitution, Congress and the Federal Executive branch said that the territory's basic status and congressional powers regarding the territory would not change with the constitution. And Puerto Rico's governor and resident commissioner acknowledged this in congressional hearings at the time.

The confusion about an alternative to statehood or nationhood really began with the constitution giving the territorial government different official names in Spanish and English and language used in documents related to the constitution's approval.

The Spanish name strongly suggested to Puerto Ricans that there was a new status. Indeed, as you know, a freely associated state is very different from a territory—and from Puerto Rico's status—in U.S. and international law. A freely associated state is a nation that associates with another in a joint governing arrangement that either can end. It has usually been a territory that associates with its former national governing power as it attains nationhood.

The constitution's English name has no real status meaning. Four States use "Commonwealth" in their official names. Another territory does as well.

Federal officials could accept the meaningless English name of "Commonwealth" but would certainly not have approved "Associated Free State," which would have misleadingly suggested nationhood.

After the constitution was adopted, officials who controlled Puerto Rico's government from the political party that did not want true nationhood or statehood told Puerto Ricans that a new status had been established. Federal officials did not agree that Puerto Rico was no longer a territory or no longer subject to Congress' territory governing power, but they did not publicly contradict and, sometimes, contributed to the misimpression to counter foreign 'Cold War' criticism of U.S. colonialism.

The 'commonwealthers' also began to try to get Federal agreement to create a new status. Thus, the Federal rejections in every decade beginning with the Fifties that I noted.

All of the "Commonwealth" proposals had the same or similar constitutional and other deficiencies, leading to the Federal rejections.

So, "Commonwealth" and the words that literally translate as "Associated Free State" in Puerto Rico misleadingly have three distinct meanings in the islands—the territorial government, Puerto Rico's current status, and the 'Commonwealth' party's proposal for a new status. The different meanings confuse Puerto Ricans as well as people outside the territory.

Under the 'Commonwealth' party's definition since 1998 for the new status, the United States would be bound to an arrangement with Puerto Rico under which the insular government could nullify the application of Federal laws and Federal court jurisdiction and the insular government could enter into international agreements and organizations that require national sovereignty.

The Federal government would also be obligated to grant the insular government a new subsidy and most of its lands in the islands and required to continue to grant all current program benefits to Puerto Ricans, U.S. citizenship, and free access to goods shipped from Puerto Rico.

Executive branch officials and congressional committee leaders—including you, Mr. Chairman, and Senator Murkowski—have said that this proposal is impossible for constitutional and other reasons during each the Clinton, George W. Bush, and Obama Administrations.

Each of these administrations recommended that Puerto Ricans choose among the Federally recognized status options. These include: statehood; independence; true nationhood in a free—that is, unilaterally terminable—association with the U.S.; and continuing territory status for a while longer.

Territory status, whether called "Commonwealth" or not, cannot resolve the status issue because it cannot provide for equal voting representation in the Federal government. As long as Puerto Rico is subject to congressional Territory Clause power, its U.S. citizens will have the right to petition for statehood. And as long as Puerto Rico is an unincorporated territory, Puerto Ricans will have the right to petition for nationhood.

Further, territory status is not supported by any of Puerto Rico's political parties or status factions. Even the "Commonwealth" party wants a fundamentally different governing arrangement than the present one; it just wants one that the Federal government cannot agree to under the Constitution and does not want to agree to because of basic United States policies and concepts. The party will only say that it accepts the current status until it can have what it wants under its false assumption that Puerto Rico is not subject to Congress' constitutional authority under the Territory Clause.

Puerto Ricans had voted on status before the past three Federal administrations recommended Puerto Ricans choose among the Federally recognized status options, but all of the votes were confused by impossible "Commonwealth" proposals.

With boycotts by the statehood and independence parties, a plebiscite in 1967 resulted in a 60% majority for a "Commonwealth" proposals different than the current governing arrangement. But, when its proposals were written as Federal legislation in the early 1970s, the bill was opposed by the President of the United States and defeated in the House subcommittee.

A second plebiscite was held in 1993. No proposal won a majority but another "Commonwealth" proposal different than the current governing arrangement obtained a slight plurality over statehood. It, too, however, was judged to not be viable by the President and U.S. House leaders.

Statehood won the most votes among the status options of a third vote in 1998 but a bare majority of the vote chose no status option. There were campaigns for not making a choice led by advocates of the current "Commonwealth" status proposal and by other neo-nationalists.

The confusion about a "Commonwealth" option other than territory status prompted President Clinton to take several actions.

One was to establish the President's Task Force on Puerto Rico's Status to make recommendations and answer questions regarding the options and process for determining the territory's ultimate status until that status is determined.

Another measure was to propose $2.5 million for a plebiscite on options proposed by Puerto Rico's tri-partisan Elections Commission that the Federal Executive branch determined were not incompatible with the Constitution and basic laws and policies of the United States. Despite quiet lobbying against the legislation by the "Commonwealth" party, it was enacted into law in 2000. The plebiscite intended for 2001 was not held, however, because a "Commonwealth" party administration in Puerto Rico knew from positions of the Clinton and Bush Administrations that the new "Commonwealth" status proposal could not be an option.

So, the President's Task Force under President Bush recommended that Congress authorize a two-question Puerto Rican referendum status choice. The threshold question was to be whether Puerto Ricans wanted the current territory status to continue. If we did not, the second question would be whether we wanted statehood or independence, with nationhood in a free association with the U.S. an additional option if Congress wanted to add it.

Under the leadership of Resident Commissioner Pierluisi, now also president of our statehood party, the House in 2010 passed a bill for a referendum similar to that recommended by the Bush Task Force. There would have been a free association option, and territory status would have been an option on the second question as well as the first.

The "Commonwealth" party opposed the legislation, calling instead for a referendum on statehood—including in testimony to this Committee.

For the past quarter century, congressional leaders and Federal Executive branch officials have consistently responded to Puerto Rican requests for legislation to enable a Puerto Rican status choice by trying to enact such a bill. All efforts—except for President Clinton's in 2000—have been blocked in Congress at the request of the "Commonwealth" party. It has ultimately lobbied to prevent any law from being enacted because all bills have chipped away at the myth that a Puerto Rican statehood petition would be rejected because of who Puerto Ricans are and because none of the bills held the potential for becoming a law that would validate the idea of a new "Commonwealth" status.

In March 2011, President Obama's Task Force on Puerto Rico's Status recommended that Puerto Ricans be enabled as soon as possible to choose among Puerto Rico's options: continued territory status; statehood; independence; and nationhood in a free association with the U.S. The Obama Task Force did not recommend a choice process but expressed "a marginal preference" for one somewhat different from that recommended by the Bush Task Force, although still in a two-question format to increase the likelihood of a definitive result.

After trying to obtain a tri-partisan agreement on a plebiscite that proved to be unachievable because of "Commonwealth" party obstructionism, Governor Luis Fortuño proposed a vote similar to that recommended by the Bush Task Force with a true free association option labeled "Sovereign Associated Free State" out of deference to the "Commonwealth" party. As Speaker of Puerto Rico's House of Representatives, I sponsored the final legislation for the plebiscite, which was enacted into law by the elected representatives of the people of Puerto Rico.

The "Commonwealth" party urged a vote for continuing territory status although it argued that Puerto Rico is not a territory despite determinations that it is subject to Congress' territory governing powers by the U.S. Supreme Court, successive presidential administrations—including the Justice and State Departments, the full U.S. House of Representatives, the leaders of both national political parties of this Committee, the Government Accountability Office, and the American Law Division of the Congressional Research Service.

The plebiscite was held in conjunction with the territory's quadrennial elections. The results were 54% against continuing territory status and 61.2% for statehood among the alternatives to it. Nationhood in a free association with the U.S. obtained 33.3% and independence 5.5%. The vote petitioned Congress and President Obama to begin the transition of Puerto Rico to equality within the country.

Having lost the plebiscite and the representative to the Federal government position, "Commonwealth" party leaders, who very narrowly won control of the governorship and Puerto Rico's Legislative Assembly in the elections, are trying to subvert the democratic process by contending that the plebiscite was unfair and arguing that it was inconclusive.

They say that the plebiscite was unfair because it termed the current status "territorial" and because it did not include their proposed new "Commonwealth" status. But these complaints fly in the face of the Federal determinations I have referenced.

They say it was inconclusive because a minority of voters did not choose among the alternatives to territory status and they assert that these blank ballots should be counted in the percentage results although the blank ballots can represent no possible status option.

The percentage results I have cited were certified by the tri-partisan Puerto Rico Elections Commission in accordance with law and common election practice. The Supreme Court of Puerto Rico, in Suárez Cáceres v. Comisión Estatal de Elecciones (CEE), 176 DPR 31, as recently as 2009, decided that blank ballots and void or not-adjudicated ballots are not to be counted for the purpose of determining majorities and the results of a race. The Court declared that

". . . such a vote may in no way be counted in order to influence or affect the result of an election, referendum or plebiscite, among other electoral events. As stated in Burdick v. Takushi, [504 U.S. 428 (1992)], '[a]ttributing to elections a more generalized expressive function would undermine the ability of States to operate elections fairly and efficiently'. " (Suárez Cáceres v. CEE, Page 74).

In fact, the idea of counting blank ballots in the determination of the results of a status plebiscite was specifically rejected in a concurrent majority opinion:

"In a future plebiscite it is reasonably possible that one proposal for a change of political status may gain over 50% of the vote total. Adjudicating blank ballots and fictional votes artificially enlarges the electoral universe and diminishes the proportion of votes validly cast for the contending proposals. This hinders and interferes with the verification of a majority mandate for a change of status in the vote canvassing. Meanwhile it would only grant the advantage of inertia to the existing condition, which would remain in place by frustrating the majority will through a distorted vote count" (Suárez Cáceres v. CEE, Page 91).

The "Commonwealth" party's argument is that those who do not participate in a free and fair election should overrule those who do. Open elections are not determined by those who do not vote.

The Obama Administration has agreed with the people of Puerto Rico rather than the "Commonwealth" party. The President's spokesman embraced the plebiscite and recognized that there were majority votes to resolve the issue and for statehood. He also said that the Congress should act to enable the Puerto Rican self-determination and that the Administration would work with Congress to this end.

Understanding that "Commonwealth" party government opposition would probably prevent the Congress as a whole from implementing the plebiscite choice, the White House and the Justice Department proposed another vote but under Federal auspices so that it would be more difficult to dispute the will of the people.

The proposal is modeled after the plebiscite legislation that the Clinton White House got enacted in 2000. $2.5 million would be provided for a plebiscite on options that would "resolve" the status issue proposed by the tri-partisan Elections Commission to the extent that the Federal Justice Department agrees with the proposed options. This would exclude the current status because a territory status cannot resolve the issue and it would, of course, exclude the proposed new "Commonwealth" status.

As a Puerto Rican, I am deeply appreciative of the actions that the Obama White House has taken on Puerto Rico's status issue. But it is very disappointing and curious that the Administration has chosen to not testify at this hearing on the plebiscite and its response despite your request, Mr. Chairman. The Administration not testifying at any congressional hearing on the issue that the President's Task Force on Puerto Rico has reported is the territory's most important and key to addressing many of the islands' toughest challenges is a failure to fulfill a responsibility of office.

Executive branch advice and perspectives are essential to the legislative process in our system of government, which separates powers. Every previous Federal administration that has been called upon to appear at hearings on the status issue has done so. The President's Task Force is co-chaired by a designee of the attorney general who can testify if it is desired that the White House co-chair not do so. The Executive order establishing the Task Force, which President Obama endorsed, requires the Task Force to answer questions and advise on the options and process for resolving Puerto Rico's status issue. The President's spokesman said that the Administration would work with the Congress to respond to the plebiscite. The Administration has a good story to tell. And there is no real political downside. It would embarrass Governor García Padilla—but telling the truth about issues is an obligation of government.

Mr. Chairman and Members, the Puerto Rico status issue is a basic question of democracy, equality, and justice. Puerto Ricans have served side-by-side with other Americans in the Armed Forces in every conflict since World War I. In battle, the sacrifice, blood, and life of Puerto Ricans is equal to that of other Americans, but in peace, at home, Puerto Ricans are second class citizens unless they move to the States—which we can freely do as U.S. citizens. In fact, almost three out of every 10 Puerto Ricans alive has obtained equality and statehood through an airline ticket simply by moving to the State. And there are 1.2 million more people of Puerto Rican origin in the States than there are people of any origin in the islands.

For decades, Puerto Ricans have been told to come back to Washington when they decided what they wanted among the possible options for the islands' status. Now, in a free, fair, open, and democratic election called by elected representatives, the people of Puerto Rico have voted to replace the territory status misleadingly known as "Commonwealth" and petition for a beginning of the transition to the equality and permanence of statehood. It is incumbent upon this Congress to act to ensure that the colonial status of Puerto Rico—inconsistent with American values—is finally replaced.

Exhibits 1–2 have been retained in committee files.

STATEMENT OF THE BOARD OF PUERTO RICANS IN MINNESOTA,** EDINA, MN

Our organization, PR MN, a political-cultural association was formed in the Twin cities of Minneapolis, St Paul, to engage in the process of discussion and negotiations underway in Congress in respect to the political status of Puerto Rico.

We favor Independence with close ties to USA or a sovereign form of government, such as Associated Republic or enhanced commonwealth. The term soberanista incorporates those options.

We have participated in past failed attempts to solve this issue, e.g. the "Young bill" in the 1990's and others.

We hope that in light of the recent plebiscite of November 2012 and the Presidential Task force recommendations, that Congress will enact legislation to move forward in resolving this issue that has engaged Puerto Rico for 115 years, taking away time, energy and resources from solving our very pressing economic and social issues.

We have the following positions on the current issue being discussed in the Senate and that will be subject of hearings in the House of Representatives when HR2000 is reviewed. We present these recommendations in a spirit of collaboration towards the solution of this old issue. We are very aware that Puerto Rico is facing great challenges in economic and social issues as well and that solution of this status issue will greatly resolve some of these, as they are in some ways a consequence of the stalemate in solving this status issue.

We "Puerto Ricans in Minnesota" want to be part of the political process occurring in Congress. The form of involvement of the Puerto Ricans living in the USA should be specified early on the negotiations and should be a high priority part of all discussions and legislations There are almost 4 million Puerto Ricans or Puerto Rican descendants outside the island, possibly 20,000 living throughout the state of Minnesota. Most of us have family there; many have real estate properties and are clear all Puerto Ricans in USA will be also affected by any status change. PR has been dealing with this issue for 115 years since we became an unincorporated territory as a result of the Spanish American War of 1898. The President's Task Force on Puerto Rico's Status, acknowledges, together with a series of official statements by U.S. authorities over the past 20 years, that Puerto Rico is an unincorporated territory of the United States under the sovereignty of the United States.

We all feel the recent status plebiscite results are being distorted and misrepresented as showing the statehood choice won when in reality, as compared to 1998, this options lost 2 %.(Data can be provided on request)

We support the independentista/soberanista options and oppose statehood. We feel statehood will cause severe economic, cultural, and linguistic disruption of a very homogeneous Latin-American culture and nationality unsurpassed in its determination to prevail. We recognize and appreciate USA assistance in solving some of our social, educational and health problems but we feel it is imperative to move out of the current state of dependency and take responsibility for all our affairs and open the way for other options of relating to this globalize world we live in the following ways: international commerce away from the current Cabotage laws, more economic and political relations with Latin America and other benefits that will open up. The current colonial form of commonwealth has no power in Congress to legislate, and the Resident Commissioner has no vote on issue that affects us. The recent vote was clearly against this form Of Commonwealth.

We recognize status options that will include two sovereign nations agreeing to share resources in an equal basis and have equal rights, e.g. Canada and the UK, and other international options to be reviewed. These forms.will be included under the umbrella term of soberanistas and can take forms such as Associated Republic or enhanced commonwealth and need to be defined clearly prior to any referendum and through a constitutional assembly to be convened.

We feel the Congress has eluded its responsibility to sponsor a process of decolonization and should act now to address this matter of status without further delay

We strongly favor a constitutional Assembly in Puerto Rico with participation of US Puerto Ricans as the best process to clearly define the formulas to be negotiated and to delineate the transition process to enact the options, especially the independence/soberanista one and then submitting these to a final island wide referendum including USA Puerto Ricans. The final referendum should be UN supervised with international observers specially from Latin-American countries...

We believe that Puerto Ricans have as much right to obtain support from the international community on its quest for independence/soberania as the US had to get support from other countries in its own Independence movements. Many times in the last 115 years the Latino Americans diverse political organization, e.g. COPPAL, i.e. Permanent conference of Latin American Political parties, and recently the Congress of Latin American and Caribbean states (CÓPAL) have expressed support for this option and in the words of President Martín Torrijos of Panama, the keynote speaker at the Latin American and Caribbean Congress in Solidarity with Puerto Rico's Independence held in Panama City in November 2006:

> "The basic problem is that Puerto Rico is the only Hispanic American nation that remains under a colonial regime. For Latin Americans, forever correcting this anomaly must be a matter of principle and a priority of continental proportions. What remains is to agree on whatever is necessary to concrete the Puerto Rican right to constitute an independent republic."

We are available to fully participate in the process under way and look forward to further interactions through the Congressional offices of our representatives from our state of Minnesota.

We further request that this statement be included in the official record of the committee on energy and natural resources scheduled for hearing on Aug 1, 2013

Respectfully submitted,

MIGUEL E. FIOL,
*coordinator,***

ELSA PÉREZ VEGA,
coordinator,

ALAN PANELLI,
MARI ISA PÉREZ,
MYRNA SUAREZ,
JUAN RUAS AND OTHERS.

———

STATEMENT OF DENNIS O. FREYTES, AMERICAN VETERAN, FORMER PROFESSOR (PMS) AND DEPARTMENT DIRECTOR UNIVERSITY OF PUERTO RICO, VP NAUS-AMERICAN VETERANS SE REGION, COMMUNITY SERVANT, NATIONAL ASSOCIATION FOR UNIFORMED SERVICES, VICE-PRESIDENT SE REGION (FL, GA, SC, AL, MS, MO, AR, & PR)

As a Patriotic statutory US Citizen, I thank this Honorable Body for allowing my factual based Testimony that strikes at the heart and essence of our American Democracy-Federal "consent of the governed"; just representation!

On behalf of millions of disfranchised loyal Americans (including American Veterans)—we respectfully ask the Federal Government to do right—promptly move to end the political oppression of 2d Class US Citizens and Veterans (mainly residing in the US Territory of Puerto Rico)—that don't have full human individual civil rights, and benefits; are facing institutional discrimination—to include no Federal Vote, just representation or un-permanent US Citizenship while under the will of Congress.

We fight for hard working and loyal patriotic US Citizens that includes my Mother-Gloria E. Gonzalez-Marrero (School Teacher & Social Worker), late Father-Celio

Freytes Menendez (a Borinqueneer Angel) who has the Combat Infantrymen's Badge w/Star (WW-II & Korea)—fought with the brave Hispanic segregated US 65th Infantry Regiment (Borinqueneers); Family, and Friends—that want a Federal Government that applies equally our "We the People" US Constitution; ends institutional Voter discrimination and segregation; is honest, fair and does right for all!

We (as other Americans) yearn for truth, equality, justice, and dignity as we pursue the American dream! Now, is the time for American Patriots (of true grit) to move Congress to enact a sanctioned Plebiscite: HR 2000-Puerto Rico's Status Resolution Act (a Statehood YES or NO Vote); redress this terrible wrong against the Soul of our American democracy! The straight facts (without political spins) are:

"Canto claro como un Gallo de Manati!"

The complex US Territory of Puerto Rico's equal rights quandary, that affects millions of discriminated US Citizens, is not only about a "Group" Vote on the status question, but, more important, it's about protecting individual civil rights in our representative democracy-where the US Citizen should be the epicenter of our Republic, not the US Government's un-democratic territorial control of the land & People. All Federal Laws and US Constitution are supreme in PR. (The Federal Government controls or oversees the currency, economy, security, borders, shipping, taxes, benefits. . . and all local laws.)

Our factual history states: in 1898, the U.S invaded Puerto Rico (PR), as part of the Spanish American War, and forcefully took it as a spoil of combat. . .made it a US Territory (Colony) that for 115+ years, falls under the absolute un-democratic control of the Federal Government (per the *U.S. Constitution Article 4, trite Territorial Clause that states: "The Congress shall have power to dispose of and make all needful Rules and Regulations respecting the Territory. . .or property belonging to the U.S.")

In 1917, Congress erred in imposing on PR-a statutory "2d Class US Citizenship" (without all rights responsibilities, & benefits) that doesn't permit loyal US Citizens (including fighting US Veterans) to vote in Federal elections (to include for their US President-Head of State) nor have just representation in the Congress that determines their destiny nor permanent US Citizenship, under our noble USA Flag—actions that conflicts with the spirit of our democracy; constitutional civil rights equality amendments!

During 1901-1922, the "Insular Cases" were decided by Federal Courts (in a racist era) that supported a biased Congress/ Federal Government contention that Puerto Rico was an "un-incorporated" US Territory (more foreign than domestic. . .); was a possession or property that belonged to the US. Thus, Congress had the un-democratic power to not fully apply the US Constitution to Puerto Rico! Till today, this unequal and un-democratic application of our Constitution results in institutional discrimination, and Voter segregation of US Citizens, depending on where US Citizens reside under our noble US Flag! The "un-incorporated" term is not found in our Constitution. It is a historic fact that some Congressmen and Federal Judges (of the time) as they coined this term—made outrageous racist and biased comments, e.g., "Because of different origin and language. . . Puerto Ricans were inferior mestizos; could not govern themselves. . ."—which incorrectly is still the basis of Federal governance of the US Territory of PR!

Many of these discriminating insular cases, the most egregious Bidwell and Balzac have not been completely overturned, but, have been sustained in modern Federal Court decisions that still uphold the right of Congress to "differentiate" (discriminate) when applying the US Constitution to PR! Where is the Patriotic outcry against an aged wrong; and where is our Federal Government (to include our US President and the US Justice Department) that have taken no action to protect individual civil rights for all? Are US Citizens from Puerto Rico-still seen to be less worthy than other US Citizens?

Former Chief Judge Torruella (US 1st Circuit Court of Appeals) in his Book-has critiqued the judicial system and compares the "Insular Cases" (1901-1922), that defined the status of Puerto Rico to Plessy v. Ferguson (separate but equal doctrine to justify racial segregation) that was overturned with Brown v Board of Education (1954)—to Puerto Rico's case of un-democratic inequality (2d Class US Citizenship).

Judge Torruella states, "The Supreme Court continues to cling to this anachronistic remnant of the stone age of American constitutional law notwithstanding that the doctrines espoused by the "Insular Cases" seriously curtail the rights of several million citizens... of the US." Reflecting on over 115+ years of US un-democratic control of Puerto Rico, Torruella further says: "the disparity of rights that result from this relationship has in my opinion for too long been relegated to the back burners of American constitutional thought and dialogue..." and "whatever the future holds for this island, its people should strive for the equality which has too long eluded them".

Current US District Judge GELPÍ, in 2008, stated in a decision: ". . .The unequal and discriminatory fiscal treatment given to Puerto Rico. . .is conspicuous and egregious. More so, it is not an isolated incident of the federal government disparately treating Puerto Rico and the nearly four million United States citizens living in or moving to this territory."

- Under the Insular Cases doctrine (Balzac vs Porto Rico-1922), the court determined that Puerto Rico was an unincorporated territory (more foreign than domestic); only fundamental constitutional rights extended to unincorporated United States territories apply, others can be denied by Congress. . .In an unincorporated United States territory Congress can also differentiate (discriminate) against the territory and its citizens so long as there exists a rational basis for such disparate treatment. Califano v. Torres, (1984); Harris v. Rosario (1980).

Per US Constitution—PR can only be: a State or Territory under the sovereignty of the US. Besides, the only Non-Territorial Statuses are: Statehood or Independence, period. But, some distort the truth to fool people—by referring to PR's Status as "Commonwealth" or translated in Spanish-ELA (Free Associated State). These terms are not found in the US Constitution! They are (no meaning) political names for a local regulated government (with some broad powers) allowed under the control of Congress.

The PR Resident Commissioner represents about 4 million US Citizens (that proportionally is equal to six US Representatives and two US Senators)—with no vote in Congress. This is not democracy!

This iconic American Hispanic civil rights issue that strikes at the Soul of our Democracy—"consent of the governed"—has not received the National attention it merits! But, now we must act with truth & fairness (no political incongruence, rhetoric or spin). . .; not stereotype, but, soar above political closet bias to advance our democracy; ensure equality; break Puerto Rico's trite Territorial un-democratic shackles!

*Note: About 5 million US Puerto Ricans have "voted with their feet"—moved to the States with more on the way. . .To help stem the flow, PR's Status issue must be promptly resolved.

Abraham Lincoln & Martin Luther King (which stood for equality; a government by & for the People) would be appalled at PR's un-equal Federal status! US President Regan said: it was an "un-natural" state (favored statehood); is among other US Presidents, Gov. Jeb Bush, Rep. Serrano, Attorney General Thornburg. . .and Others that are for ending a 2d Class US Citizenship; un-democratic Territorial Status.

Moving forward, PR held an internal plebiscite (Nov. 2012). Results: 54% (958,915) —end Territorial Status; 61+% (824,195) Statehood; 5% (74,812) Independence. . . (Voted: 78%-See Notes below.)

However, the political misinformation, and misinterpretation of the results have begun; some are trying to discredit a democratic Plebiscite where everyone had the opportunity and duty to vote. These crafty Politicians don't want some ballots (left in blank) to count; try to impossibly divine how People would vote! The plebiscite results were clear—a Non-Territorial Status through Statehood won as duly ratified by the PR's Elections Commission. The People's democratic Vote (within the law) must be respected by all!

After 115+ years of non-action, the Federal Government must not cloud the truth or give excuses, but, promptly intervene to protect all individual civil rights; end an un-democratic Federal Territorial Status that goes against the grain of our American democracy; enact HR-2000 ("Puerto Rico Status Resolution Act"—yes or no vote on Statehood); ratify any free majority decision for Statehood; start the transition process (which should not take more than 3-5 years) to admit Puerto Rico as the 51st State of our Union.

In the final analysis, the duty of the Federal Government (which at times has been benevolent) is to: educate; end political discrimination; enact HR 2000 or at least conduct a self-determined Plebiscite with honest constitutionally non-territorial defined Options (that don't fool people); achieve political equality:

- Statehood (US Citizenship & US Constitution; PR State Sovereignty and Identity)
- Independence (PR Citizenship & PR Constitution; loss of protection of US Constitution). *Associate Independence: Free Association or ELA Soberano—are

forms of Independence because a Nation can't be sovereign or enact a pact when under the loyalty, Citizenship & Constitution of another Nation.)

- The US Territory option should not be in play because it is un-democratic; contains a Puerto Rican rejected repressive dinosaur statutory 2d Class US Citizenship; is incongruent/ conflicts with equal civil rights amendments of the US Constitution; our representative democracy.
- Let all statutory US Citizens (born in PR) vote (no matter the residency) because the outcome affects them (have "standing")—could lose their, under the will of Congress, un-permanent US Citizenship.
- A Pact can contain certain benefits. . .; but, it surrenders certain sovereign rights until the Pact is terminated by either side; with no opportunity for Statehood or permanent US Citizenship.

MACRO CONTRIBUTIONS INCLUDE

US Puerto Ricans are the 2d largest US Hispanic segment of our US population-about 9 million strong with most residing in the States (5m) & 4m in PR—whose Ancestors (roots/ heritage) led to the discovery of Florida; brought advance civilization (of the times), Christianity, Horses, Cattle, Pigs. . . to the settlement of the USA—107 years before the Pilgrims landed. . . Plus, Puerto Ricans supported and fought in the US War of Independence with General George Washington; Civil War...

Puerto Rico (with more population than 24 States) is the oldest Territory in US History; has bravely defended the US Flag to include the US 65th Infantry Regiment (Borinqueneers-since 1898) that suffered segregation, discrimination, and unequal US Citizenship, yet, bravely fought for all of us. Its Colors were passed to the PR National Guard which is serving, along with other Patriots from PR, in the Global War on Terrorism. They loyally sacrifice; fight. . . shed blood in defending the US—for the good of all.

General of the Armies (5 Stars) Douglas MacArthur once said: ". . .the Puerto Ricans. . .of the gallant 65th Infantry on the battlefields of Korea by valor, determination and a resolute will to victory give daily testament to their invincible loyalty to the United States. . .They write a brilliant record of achievement in battle and I am proud indeed to have them in this command. I wish that we might have many more like them!"

PR is a valuable US Territory, with an educated bi-lingual Work Force, that serves, among other things, as a unique open market that fuels about one million American jobs; buys about $21 billion in US Goods & Services; is the US world's eighth trading partner, and 4th largest purchaser of goods (buys more products from the U.S. mainland than many larger countries such as Italy, Russia or China). Also, it's an important defense outpost, a big pool for recruiting military personnel; a pharmaceutical, Microsoft Computer Programs, and other Industries' center of Excellence!

US Citizens in PR, like other States, are a very complex group of people that are legally born US Citizens-part of our US multi-ethnic and beautiful "Tapestry" of vibrant colors that is united and bonded together by loyalty to our US Constitution; common values, a yearn for Liberty and pursuit of the American dream. They are very proud of their roots, linage, and heritage as part of the shared macro Western culture. Plus, as most enlighten US Citizens, they believe in: God, love, truth, fairness, justice, democracy, freedom. . .; are hard workers, family oriented; community servants. . .—US values engrained!

Don't align with those that misinform, stereotype, or make biased excuses (e.g. culture, language, consensus. . .) or maintain the colonial mindset. PR has the same macro-culture as other States. More Spanish is spoken in the States than in Puerto Rico! (The US is among the largest Spanish Nation in the World; has no official language; is a land of Immigrants that comes together for the good of all!)

Each State has its own sovereignty, identity, diversity, and unique customs, so, should Puerto Rico—who's loyal US Citizens, deserve the same rights as all! We must stop institutional discrimination; the mal-interpretation of our modern Constitution. Our Nation is formed by the union of States focused on Equality (protected civil rights), Justice, Liberty. . .for the good of all!

EQUALITY NOW!

We now own our Constitution; not our fore Fathers! If there are constitutional contradictions—conflict between the old un-democratic Territorial clause (land domain laws) and the Bill of Rights and other equality amendments, the Federal Courts should favor individual civil rights. . .; ensure the US Citizen is the focus of our democracy...Plus, the 14th Amendment states that you are a US Citizen if you are born in a State or Naturalized. (Statehood is the only Status that guarantees equal & permanent US Citizenship.)

The President/Federal Government/Justice Department should move to clearly overturn the US Supreme Court Balzac decision (1922) which is to US Citizens in Puerto Rico what Plessy v. Ferguson ("separate but equal" doctrine) was to African Americans before Brown v. Board of Education. Let's not be incongruent-the US Constitution should equally apply to all US Citizens residing in PR; under our grand USA Flag! If not, there is discrimination; voter segregation. . .—no Federal consent of the governed!

In the interim, until institutional equality is achieved and the Status issue is promptly resolved: Congress must incorporate PR; provide more representation, allow six Territory Representatives (TR) with full vote in the US House (proportional to the population) which isn't prohibited by our Constitution...

In the long range, amend the US Constitution to ensure it is not left to misinterpretation that once you acquire a US Citizenship it isn't under the will of Congress, but, under the will of the People's US Constitution-with permanency, full rights, responsibilities, and benefits! Let us truly set a world shining example of a great Nation under a representative democracy for all!

A representative Government should serve the People, not be their Master; unfairly subjugate them with no right to just representation in Congress. There is no true democracy without equal representation; protected individual civil rights. Even if one US Citizen can't Vote. . .it is one too many! The original Territorial Clause was written in another biased era. . .when the founding Fathers (with no Women, Blacks, or Hispanics participation; some had slaves) brought a wondrous general democracy, but, were more focused on uniting sovereign States; organizing a Federal Government and US boundaries. . . Thus, based on the times, they didn't focus the US Constitution on the US Citizen (with equal rights). Now, our democracy has evolved with its amendments! Today, US Citizenship equality (per the US Constitution's Amendments/ Bill of Rights) is more important. We now own our US Constitution; let's make it better!

Now it's time for bold leadership; Patriots with true grit must rise to the occasion! Individual Civil Rights are totemic to our democracy; must be protected against "Federal political oppression" or like former US Patriots said, the "tyranny of a majority"! Territories are undemocratic dinosaurs of our trite colonial past!

Congress with truth, fairness, & justice must promptly do right: ensure equal US Citizenship; per the People's determination—admit the US Territory of Puerto Rico as the 51st State of the Union or give them Independence! True Patriots shall overcome! Please, ponder this—

Patriotic Question: If you support the essence of our Democracy-consent of the governed (just representation); an equal US Citizenship & just application of the US Constitution; protected individual civil rights; ending political discrimination under our US Flag, then, will you heed the truth; take prompt action to end a non-permanent "2d Class US Citizenship" (that affects millions of US Citizens-including fighting American Veterans that can't Vote); end political oppression and the trite undemocratic Status of the US Territory of Puerto Rico; advance American Democracy; ensure equal US Citizenship?

THANKS for the great things you do for the good of all: Family, Community, USA, and Humanity!

* SUMMARY

Based on the facts, (e.g. Insular Cases-Balzac; Harris vs Rosario; other Cases; Reports):

1. Based the racist Insular Cases: Congress can differentiate (discriminate); not apply equally the US Constitution to the US Citizens in PR. . .which goes against the grain of our representative democracy.

2. The US Supreme Court hasn't decided a case or Congress hasn't written any clear laws to refute: Puerto Rico is an un-incorporated (foreign) US Territory...

3. US Citizens born in Puerto Rico are not covered by the 14th Amendment. . . Thus, they don't have a permanent US Citizenship. (Naturalization may only be applied in a State, not on foreign land of an un-incorporated Territory which belongs to the US but it is not a part of it...) Individuals born in Puerto Rico are not US Citizens by virtue of the Constitution of the US, instead they are 2d Class US Citizens by revocable laws of the US Congress.

4. A Future Congress can revoke the Laws or is not bind by a previous Congress, thus the US Citizenship permanency of all born in Puerto Rico is in question. . .

5. Most US Citizens born in Puerto Rico have a statutory 2d Class non-permanent US Citizenship, no matter where they reside under our American Flag. . .

Enclosures* (Facts & Back-up Notes follows.)

STATEMENT OF EMILIO PANTOJAS-GARCÍA[†]

THE PUERTO RICO STATUS QUESTION: CAN THE STALEMATE BE BROKEN?[‡]

The result of what has been said is that while in an international sense Porto Rico was not a foreign country, since it was owned by the United States, it was foreign to the United States in a domestic sense, because the island had not been incorporated into the United States but was merely appurtenant thereto as a possession. Justice Edward Douglas White U.S. Supreme Court, 1901[1]

Finally, at the Herat of this Report and central to the lives of many Puerto Ricans, is the issue of the political status of Puerto Rico. I am firmly committed to the principle that the question of political status is a matter of self-determination the people of Puerto Rico...Both the President and Congress have roles to play to help Puerto Rico settle its future status; I am committed to working with Congress to ensure that a fair, clearly defined and transparent process is available for the people of Puerto Rico to decide on their future for themselves.
George W. Bush
Report by The President's Task force on the Puerto Rico Status. March 2011

Since the United States invasion of Puerto Rico on July 25, 1898, the Island experienced several changes in its political system from a military government to the current Estado Libre Asociado (Free Associated State), known in English as Commonwealth. Yet, as the above quotes—one hundred and ten years apart—reveal, the Island continues to be a possession of the United States: an unincorporated territory that belongs to, but it is not part of that nation. While the United States sought to present the creation of a "Commonwealth" as an act of political self determination and was able to remove Puerto Rico from the United Nations' list of non-independent territories, the status question continues to be the key axis of Puerto Rican politics and U.S.—Puerto Rico relations.

This essay shall address three issues: why does the status question continue unresolved; what is the current status of the "status question"; and finally, can the stalemate on this issue be surmounted.

A BRIEF HISTORICAL BACKGROUND

Puerto Rico became a colony of the United States as a result of the Spanish-Cuban-American War of 1898. Along with Puerto Rico, Cuba and the Philippines came under American sovereignty. From 1898 to 1900 Puerto Rico was ruled by a military government.

In 1900, with the passage of the Foraker Act (officially the Organic Act of 1900), Puerto Rico was afforded a civilian government. The U.S President appointed a civilian governor, all cabinet members and a Resident Commissioner to the U.S. Congress. An 11 member Executive Council was established. All members of the Council were appointed by the U.S. President: five individuals were selected from Puerto Rico residents while the rest were from those in top cabinet positions, including the Island's attorney general and the chief of police. The Act provided for a House of Representatives with 35 members elected from the local political parties. A Judicial system with a Supreme Court was also established, with all judges appointed by the U.S. President. All federal laws of the United States were to be in effect on the Island and thus a United States (Federal) District Court was also established. Puerto

---

*Enclosures have been retained in committee files.
† Senior Researcher and Professor of Sociology, Center for Social Research, University of Puerto Rico, Río Piedras. emilio.pantojas@upr.edu. Thanks to my research assistant, Luis J. Cintrón Gutiérrez, of the Graduate Program in Sociology at University of Puerto Rico, Río Piedras.
‡ Paper presented at the 38th Annual Conference of the Caribbean Studies Association, Panel 15 A, What future for the Non-Sovereign Caribbean?, Grenada, W.I. June 7, 2013.
[1] Quoted in Christina Duffy Burnett and Burke Marshal (eds.), Foreign in a Domestic Sense: Puerto Rico, American Expansion and the Constitution (Durham, London: Duke University Press, 2001), 13.

Rican citizenship was created thus making Puerto Ricans "foreign in a domestic sense."

In 1917, the Jones Act provided a new legal framework to Puerto Rico U.S.—relations. American citizenship was granted to Puerto Ricans, an elected Senate was created and the Resident Commissioner would now be elected as well. The Act also provided a Bill of Rights and maintained the elected House of Representatives. As Puerto Ricans became U.S. citizens by statute, they could be conscripted into the U.S. armed forces but could not run for president, even if they resided in the United States.

No major changes to the Jones Act were made until 1946. With the creation of the United Nations and the imminent decolonization processes to dismantle the old empires after WWII, the United States President Harry S. Truman appointed the first Puerto Rican governor and later Congress passed a law allowing for the election of the Puerto Rican governor, which came in effect in 1948. Thus by 1948 the basis of the "Commonwealth" status formula was in place: locally elected government with a republican form (three branches), U.S. citizenship and a bill of rights. Between 1950 and 1952 the U.S. Congress dealt with the Puerto Rican status question by enacting a new "Federal Relations Act" (Public Law 600) that replaced the Jones Act, and providing for a process for Puerto Ricans to form a Constitutional Assembly in order to write a local constitution fashioned after, and subject to, the Constitution of the United States and the approval of Congress. After changes were made by the U.S. Congress, a referendum was held on March 3, 1952 and eighty-one percent of the electorate supported the creation of the Estado Libre Asociado and the new Constitution.

Much has been said about the fact that the Nationalist Party, which opposed Commonwealth as a "colonial ploy" to free the United States from United Nations supervision on Puerto Rico, was repressed previous to the 1952 plebiscite. The fact of the matter is that many nationalist were imprisoned and a "gauge law" was passed prohibiting seditious speech previous to the Commonwealth plebiscite in 1952. The participation rate in this plebiscite was 54.7 per cent; the lowest in any status consultation. In 1953, the United States government informed the UN that Puerto Rico had exercised its right to self determination. Following the report, UN resolution 748 (VIII) recognized Puerto Rico as an autonomous, non dependent territory with self government and associated to the United States, thus removing the Island from the list of non-independent territories and exempting the United States from reporting on its status and affairs.

A special issue of The Annals of the American Academy of Political and Social Science was published in January 1953 to present and celebrate this new form of government as a showcase for democracy for the world's "dependent areas". The volume included contributions by major academic and political figures involved in the making of Commonwealth such as: Governor Luis Muñoz Marín, head of the Economic Development Administration Teodoro Moscoso, Economist John K. Galbraith and Harvard law professors Karl Friedrich and Rupert Emerson, among others.[2] In his article "Puerto Rico and American Policy toward Dependent Areas" Emerson stated:

> [T]he most distinctive element is that they [the Puerto Rican people] now have for the first time in their history given themselves a constitution and given their consent to their relationship to the United States (...) It is arguable that the status which they now have does not differ greatly in substance from that which they had before; but to press that argument too far would be to ignore the great symbolic effect of entering into a compact with the United States and governing themselves under an instrument of their own fashioning. . .(p. 10)

THE STALEMATE

Within seven years of the creation of Commonwealth, the very government that fashioned it was requesting "cosmetic" changes to Law 600. In spite of all the maneuvers, the world and many Puerto Ricans continued to denounce the Island status as colonial. The Fernós-Murray Bill was introduced in Congress in 1959 to enact those cosmetic changes. This would be the first of over a dozen bills that throughout the years "died" in Committee or were rejected by one of the chambers of Congress not making it to the next.

---

[2] The volume concluded with the text of the Constitution of the Commonwealth of Puerto Rico. The ANNALS of the American Academy of Political and Social Science January 1953, 285. http://ann.sagepub.com/content/285/1.toc

50

Since 1959 there have been three noteworthy initiatives in Washington to modify the Puerto Rico status. Two of these initiatives came from the U.S. President and occurred in the context of major shifts on inter-American policy. The first Came from the Kennedy Administration and was linked to the Alliance for Progress. The Alliance was a policy shift to counter the potential spread of socialist revolutions throughout Latin America. At a White house reception held on March 13, 1961 to announce the initiative to Latin American Diplomats and members of Congress Kennedy stated:

> As a citizen of the United States let me be the first to admit that we North Americans have not always grasped the significance of this common mission, just as it is also true that many in your own countries have not fully understood the urgency of the need to lift people from poverty and ignorance and despair. But we must turn from these mistakes—from the failures and the misunderstandings of the past—to a future full of peril but bright with hope.

> [. . .]Therefore I have called on all the people of the hemisphere to join in a new Alliance for Progress—Alianza para [el] Progreso—a vast cooperative effort, unparalleled in magnitude and nobility of purpose, to satisfy the basic needs of the American people for homes, work and land, health and schools—techo, trabajo y tierra, salud y escuela.

> [. . .]To achieve this goal political freedom must accompany material progress. Our Alliance for Progress is an alliance of free governments-and it must work to eliminate tyranny from a hemisphere in which it has no rightful place. Therefore let us express our special friendship to the people of Cuba and the Dominican Republic—and the hope they will soon rejoin the society of free men, uniting with us in our common effort.[3]

This event took place a month before the failed Bay of Pigs invasion, and a few years before the second American invasion of the Dominican Republic. The treaty creating the Alliance for Progress was signed in Punta del Este, Uruguay in August 1961. In November of that year, Teodoro Moscoso (the architect of Puerto Rico's Operation Bootstrap) was appointed coordinator of the Alliance and Regional Administrator for Latin America of the United States International Agency for Development (USAID). On December 1961, after breaking relations with Cuba, President Kennedy traveled to Latin America to promote the Alliance, visiting San Juan, Caracas and Colombia. Governor of Puerto Rico Luis Muñoz Marín was a key to Kennedy's new Latin American policy, being part of what at the time was called "the democratic left" in Latin America.

As a reward for the services of the Government of Puerto Rico in launching the Alliance, President Kennedy sent the following message to Governor Muñoz Marín for the celebration of the tenth anniversary of Commonwealth on July 25, 1962.[4]

> The achievements of the Puerto Rican people in this short period have been remarkable. Puerto Rico has furnished an example to the world of the benefits that can be achieved by close collaboration between a larger and a smaller community within the framework of freedom and mutual agreement. I am confident that I speak for the people of the United States as well as their government in expressing my pride and pleasure at Puerto Rico's achievements.

> I am aware, however, as you point out, that the Commonwealth relationship is not perfected and that it has not yet realized its full potential, and I welcome your statement that the people of Puerto Rico are about to begin the consideration of this with the purpose of moving towards its maximum development. I am in full sympathy with this aspiration. I see no reason why the Commonwealth concept, if that is the desire of the people of Puerto Rico, should not be fully developed as a permanent institution in its association with the United States. I agree that this is a proper time to recognize the need for growth and, both as a matter of fairness to all concerned and of establishing an unequivocal record, to consult the people of Puerto

[3] Modern History Sourcebook: "President John F. Kennedy: On the Alliance for Progress", 1961.http://www.fordham.edu/halsall/mod/1961kennedy-afp1.html (May 16, 2013).
[4] Note that the date of the creation of Commonwealth coincides with the day of the U.S. invasion of Puerto Rico, July 25. All dates quoted previously come from: New York Times Chronology, 1961.http://www.jfklibrary.org/Research/Research-Aids/Ready-Reference/New-York-Times-Chronology/Browse-by-Date/New-York-Times-Chronology-December-1961.aspx (May 16, 2013).

Rico, as you propose to do, so that they may express any other preference, including independence, if that should be their wish.[5]

After the assassination of President Kennedy, all hopes for a reform of Law 600 and the enhancement of the Commonwealth autonomy through Presidential and Congressional action were dampened. This eventually led to the 1967 plebiscite as a strategy of Commonwealth supporters, who had been in power since 1940, to put pressure for change on Washington. Yet, President Lyndon B. Johnson refused to meet with the Puerto Rico Secretary of State, who was to deliver personally the results of the plebiscite.[6]

The second major Washington initiative to resolve the Puerto Rico status question came from President George H.W. Bush in 1989. In the context of the Enterprise of the Americas Initiative which eventually became the Free Trade Areas of the Americas (FTAA) initiative. In his first State of the Union Address President Bush called on Congress to act on Puerto Rico's political future.

> There's another issue that I've decided to mention here tonight. I've long believed that the people of Puerto Rico should have the right to determine their own political future. Personally, I strongly favor statehood. But I urge the Congress to take the necessary steps to allow the people to decide in a referendum.[7]

The President's request resulted in the introduction on April 4, 1989 of the "Puerto Rico Status Referendum Act" (S. 712). As chair of the Senate Committee on Energy and Natural Resources, which is charged to deal with issues relating to the U.S. possessions, Senator Bennett Johnston held extensive hearings. For the first time since the enactment of Law 600 and the creation of Commonwealth, Congress embarked in a process of hearings and substantial deliberations on the Puerto Rico status question. The process was so inclusive that the leader of the Puerto Rican Independence Party expressed great satisfaction with the fact that Congress provided for the first time in history a viable and mutually agreeable definition of independence. Various books were later written about what was termed the process of negotiations and consultations of 1989-1990.[8] In reality these were Congressional Hearings, but not accustomed to openness and exchange of views with members of Congress, the local politicians and pundits thought they had participated in "consultations and negotiations." They were promptly disabused as the bill was not approved in the 101st Congress. Reintroduced as in the Senate as S. 244 in the 102nd Congress, the bill "failed to approve" in the Committee of Energy and Natural Resources, never making it to the Senate floor or the House.

The last noteworthy attempt to provide for a congressionally sanctioned solution to the Puerto Rico status question was the introduction of the "United States-Puerto Rico Political Status Act" by Alaska Republican Don Young (H.R. 3024 in the 104th Congress and H.R. 856 in the 105th congress). Although the bill was passed in the House 209 to 208 votes; it was referred to the Senate (S. 472) and never made it to the Senate's floor.

THE 2012 PLEBISCITE: PROSPECTS FOR A SOLUTION?

The latest of the four status plebiscites sent two clear messages: (1) the majority of Puerto Ricans are dissatisfied with Commonwealth; (2) there is a growing number of Puerto Ricans—although still a minority—that favor a "sovereign free associated state" or a more autonomous Commonwealth. The ballot for this plebiscite was divided in two parts. On the first part voters were asked: Do you agree that Puerto Rico should continue to have its present form of territorial status? The results were 54 per cent "no" and 46 per cent "yes", a clear rejection of the current status. But when given three choices on the second part of the ballot, statehood, independence and sovereign free associated state ("sovereign Commonwealth"), the results did not yield a clearly favored alternative. Table 1 summarizes the results of the four plebiscites and puts in perspective the difficulty of solving the status question.

---

[5] John F. Kennedy: "Message to Governor Munoz Marin on the 10th Anniversary of the Commonwealth of Puerto Rico." July 25, 1962. Online by Gerhard Peters and John T. Woolley, The American Presidency Project. http://www.presidency.ucsb.edu/ws/?pid=8787 (May 16, 2013).

[6] Angel Collado Schwarz, "El mensaje a la metrθpolis". El Nuevo Dφa. 25 de Octubre de 2012. http://www.elnuevodia.com/columna-elmensajealametropolis-1370349.html (May 16, 2013).

[7] George H.W. Bush, "State of the Union Address," February 9, 1989. http://stateoftheunion.onetwothree.net/texts/19890209.html (May 16, 2013).

[8] Cf. Rubén Berríos-Martínez, Nacionalidad y Plebiscito (San Juan: Editorial Libertad, n.d.), 133; Juan M. García Passalacqua and Carlos Rivera Lugo, Puerto Rico y los Estados Unidos: El Proceso De Consulta Y Negociación de 1989 y 1990 (San Juan: n.p., 1991), 2 Vols.

garcia.eps

Since 1967 Commonwealth has consistently lost support. Although it got the majority vote in 1993 it failed to reach the 50 percent mark. The 1998 and 2012 plebiscites were organized and held under the pro statehood governments of the New Progressive Party (NPP). Pro Commonwealth leaders argue that the definitions crafted by the PNP legislature for that formula were distorted in order to favor statehood; hence, the "unfavorable" results in the last two plebiscites for Commonwealth. In 1998, pro Commonwealth and pro independence voters formed a coalition that introduced the alternative "none of the above" to the ballot, thus rejecting the maneuvers of the NPP government to tilt the vote in favor of statehood. The former proved to be the winning alternative, garnering 50.3 percent of the vote, thus sending the message to Congress that the Puerto Rican electorate was not sure of what it wanted but that it was not statehood, which got 46.5 percent of the vote.

The 2012 plebiscite suffered from similar maneuvering. Arguing that Commonwealth was merely a territorial status, the ballot was split as we explained earlier. As the plebiscite was held on the same day of the general elections, the status campaign overlapped with that of the political parties vying for office. The leader of the pro Commonwealth Popular Democratic Party (PPD) thus asked its supporters to vote "yes" on the first part of the ballot (supporting Commonwealth) and to leave blank the second part as a sign of protest. The results of the election were a victory for the PPD over the NPP. On the plebiscite, the current form of Commonwealth was rejected while statehood achieved a pyrrhic victory.

Although statehood got the most votes of any alternative on the second part of the ballot, 44.4 percent, the blank votes combined with the votes for "sovereign free associated state" amounted to 50.7 percent. Moreover, the share of votes for statehood decreased by 2.1 percent from 1998. The pro statehood leadership argued to no avail that statehood had won by 61 percent, as the blank votes for the second part of the ballot should not be counted to certify the results. Yet, as these were "protest votes", they became part of the calculations in spite of the protestations of the NPP leadership.

Chart 1* better illustrates the tendencies in the four plebiscites. There are two steady tendencies, one at the bottom of the chart, independence, and another at the top of the chart, statehood. Neither has grown much in the 46 years since the 1967 plebiscite. Statehood went form an initial 39 percent in 1967, to a high 46.5 percent in 1998, and down to 44.6 percent in 2012. Independence hovers at the bottom and has never reached the 5 percent mark. Commonwealth is clearly loosing support, as the results of the first part of the 2012 plebiscite demonstrate, but "sovereign Commonwealth" seems to be on the rise, gathering 24.2 percent of the vote, up form 0.3 percent in 1998.

In the absence of a clearly favored alternative, the U.S. Congress and President remained silent on the 2012 plebiscite. Finally, on April 2013 the White House announced the allocation of "$2,500,000 for objective, nonpartisan voter education about, and a plebiscite on, options that would resolve Puerto Rico's future political status, which shall be provided to the State Elections Commission of Puerto Rico: Provided, that funds provided for the plebiscite under the previous proviso shall not be obligated until 45 days after the Attorney General notifies the Committees on Appropriations that he approves of an expenditure plan from the Commission for voter education and plebiscite administration, including approval of the plebiscite ballot; Provided further, that the notification shall include a finding that the voter

---

* Chart has been retained in committee files.

education materials, plebiscite ballot, and related materials are not incompatible with the Constitution and laws and policies of the United States [sic]."[9]

Following the President's action, Puerto Rico's Resident Commissioner to the House of Representatives and NPP leader, Pedro Pierliusi presented the bill HR 2000 the "Puerto Rico Status Resolution Act", proposing a statehood "yes" or "no" plebiscite. After loosing face with the claim that statehood "won" the 2012 plebiscite with 61 percent of the vote, the statehood leader and new president of the NPP, seems to be willing to "roll the dice" in an all or nothing gamble. As Puerto Rican Congressman José Serrano warned, if a vote for statehood is lost, this alternative will be sidetracked for at least a generation.

But given the fact that Congress has not acted on any of the more than a dozen status bills presented since 1952, this gamble may prove to be superfluous. Moreover, Republicans hold the majority in the House and they have traditionally opposed statehood for Puerto Rico because: (1) the Island is culturally a Latin American Spanish speaking nation, merely 10 percent of the Puerto Ricans living on the Island are fully bilingual according to the 2010 U.S. Census; (2) the political allegiance of Puerto Ricans is to the Democratic Party, which would add two Senators and five or six Representatives for that party. To these reasons, new ones have been added: The government of Puerto Rico is nearly bankrupt; the Island's GDP has dropped over 10 percent in the past decade; unemployment was 16 percent in 2012; migration to the mainland is at a rate of 35,000 annually and the population dropped by 2 percent between the 2000 and 2010 population censuses. Some pundits argue that Puerto Rico would be a "beggar state" and a burden to Federal finances at a time of fiscal duress.

It is reasonable to conclude that, with these measures, both President Obama and Resident Commissioner Pierluisi are simply posturing to satisfy political promises made to their constituents. It is unlikely that Congress will act on any of these two proposals, and the stalemate shall continue.

————

SOCIETY FOR AMERICAN VALUES AND ENLIGHTENMENT IN PUERTO RICO, SAN JUAN, PR

(INTRODUCTION)

My name is José Garriga-Picó and I appear in representation of the Society for American Values and Enlightenment in Puerto Rico (SAVE PR), a non-partisan civil society group of citizens committed to the protection and promotion of American values and interests in Puerto Rico. Currently, I am professor of Political Science at the University of Puerto Rico where I have taught since 1979 with brief interludes at the National Autonomous University of Mexico, Boston University and Northeastern University. From 2005 to 2008, I was at large state senator in Puerto Rico. I am a Toll Fellow of the Council of State Governments. I currently do not occupy any political office.

(THE IMPORTANCE OF THE NOVEMBER 6, 2012 PLEBISCITE)

The protection of American values and interests in Puerto Rico requires that the Senate acts forthrightly on the results of the November 6, 2012 Plebiscite which elevated the question of the status of Puerto Rico to the national agenda. Said results were a clear victory for the "NO" option in the first part of the ballot. (See Appendix 1.)* The meaning of such a vote is that the American citizens living in Puerto Rico have rejected the continuation of the territorial condition to which they consented by referendum in 1951.

In 1776, our forefathers declared the independence of our original thirteen colonies based on the fact that King George III had violated the principle of government by the consent of the governed. The Puerto Rican electorate served notice last November that they do not wish to continue being governed in the way and through the institutions and laws that, by their own accord, govern them currently. That is the American way of bringing about political change. The Senate of the United States, taking the respect for the wishes of the electorate as a core American political value, has a duty to act expeditiously to insure that these democratically expressed wishes are respected and implemented. Anything short of that would not live up to our blessed principle of government by consent of the governed.

————

[9] "Puerto Rico Status Vote Proposed by White House", The Huffington Post. April 10, 2013. http://www.huffingtonpost.com/2013/04/10/puerto-rico-status-vote_n_3056579.html (May 16, 2013).

* Appendix 1–2 have been retained in committee files.

The request for the end of the current status, of course, Brings us to the question of what it should be substituted with. The wish of the American citizens who voted on this question was clear: Congress should admit Puerto Rico in the Union on an equal footing with all the other states. That has been historically the American way with all the territories that have been under the American flag for more than a hundred years. That is what the hundreds of thousands of Puerto Ricans who have fought side by side with their fellow American citizens in all our wars of the twentieth and twenty first century deserve. Simply put, statehood, for American citizens, is the American way.

(THE IDEOLOGIES OF THE POLITICAL SECTORS IN PUERTO RICO)

There should be no dispute in this Senate or in Puerto Rico that in response to the results of the plebiscite, this Senate should proceed to approve an enabling act to admit Puerto Rico to the Union but I would be professionally remiss if I failed to recognize that there are persons in Puerto Rico that do not consider themselves Americans and hence do not favor statehood.

There is a diversity of groups of this persuasion. Some simply hate the USA, and, will take sides with any party that attacks our country and its institutions. Unfortunately, as the events in the mainland have made well aware, there are many non Puerto Rican persons and groups all across our great nation that also feel and act that way. And yet, we still respect their freedom of expression and their right to the protection of their civil rights. That is the American way.

Other groups and persons (in Puerto Rico as in other territories and states), even when they are citizens, they don't feel or identify themselves as Americans but cherish the identity of the "old country". In the mainland, these persons form ghettos, in Puerto Rico they favor independence and are a very small part of the population.

A somewhat larger group of voters do not favor statehood because of the language barrier yet fear greatly losing their American citizenship and the economic consequences of not being part of the American economy. Hence they favor continuation of the current status or free association in the style the Republic of Palau, an option which most of the public fail to comprehend in all aspects. For example, the promoters of free association and even those of independence claim that they will retain American citizenship, American currency, American military protection and free access to jobs and schools in all the states even after Puerto Rico becomes sovereign.

The majority of the population feels that Puerto Rico should become a state as reflected in the plebiscite results and other independent polls because as Puerto Rican Americans they want they Island to be forever part of the Union.

(THE OBJECTIONS)

Persons and groups who do not identify themselves with America and its values object the results of the plebiscite mostly because they do not believe that the status of Puerto Rico should decided by means of a plebiscite not only because they do not share American democratic values but because they realize that they do not have the support of the majority of voters. Hence they promote the Constitutional Assembly, an instrument made popular in Latin America by Hugo Chavez to promote political change. And yet, whenever they have had the opportunity to legislate such assembly they have shrunk from doing because, ultimately, they do not want any change in the present territorial condition.

It is for this very same reason that they do not want the Congress to legislate to sponsor a plebiscite in Puerto Rico regarding status options. This also explains why they want complicated ballots with many alternatives which tend towards stalemate and inconclusive and even contradictory results. It is for this reason that they try to confound the interpretation of the results of the November 6, 2012 plebiscite.

Whatever they allege regarding these results on fact is clear: Statehood obtained more votes than any other option. Indeed it obtained a hefty majority among those who casted a vote among the status options in the second part of the ballot. They argue, however, that contrary to the American tradition unmarked ballots should be counted as favoring a particular option, the status quo, which is politically unacceptable and juridically void. But even accepting for the sake of argument their allegation that these non-votes should be counted as part of the base, it would be un-American to make the loser a winner arguing that the real winner only attained a plurality. By all counts, statehood won.

(RULES OF INTERPRETATION)

In part the confusion created based on the plebiscite results is due to a lack of firm principles of interpretation of the results in the local law that mandated it. To try to prevent confusion, even before the plebiscite, I appeared in representation of LULAC in front of members and staff of the Presidential Task Force on the Status of Puerto Rico and presented them a "Suggested Interpretation and Action Policy Regarding the Possible Results of The Plebiscite on Puerto Rico's Status of 2012". (See Appendix 2) After the plebiscite, I again returned to the Task Force, representing LULAC, to interpret the result according to the criteria I had proposed before the event. (See Appendix 3) My conclusions were that same what I am presenting here: The People of Puerto Rico voted for change in their status; they selected statehood as their preferred options for change. It is now up to the Congress to pick up the ball and continue the process of ascertaining how that change will occur.

(CONCLUSION)

Affirming that statehood won the plebiscite is a different question from saying that the Congress has to admit Puerto Rico to the Union without further consultation. In the American history and tradition admission of states has been the product of political processes of negotiation between the citizens in the territory and the Congress. What the victory of Statehood in the plebiscite means is that the American citizens in Puerto Rico are ready to begin negotiating the terms of admission. In this process, Congress should ask the People of Puerto Rico to confirm their choice of statehood in a federally mandated referendum to vote statehood up or down. I feel that HR2000 (Pierluisi Bill) in the house is an adequate model to do this. The Senate should promptly introduce and consider a similar bill to begin the process of hearings on the matter.

STATEMENT OF THE ALLIANCE FOR SOVEREIGN FREE ASSOCIATION (ALIANZA PRO LIBRE ASOCIACIÓN SOBERANA); REFERRED TO AS ALAS

THE RIGHTFUL REPRESENTATIVE OF THE FREE ASSOCIATION ALTERNATIVE

The Alliance for Sovereign Free Association (Alianza pro Libre Asociación Soberana or ALAS) is a non-partisan citizens organization dedicated to the decolonization of Puerto Rico, via the adoption of a treaty of free association between Puerto Rico and the United States of America. In 2012 ALAS was certified by the Puerto Rico Elections Commission to represent the option Sovereign Free Associated State (Estado Libre Asociado Soberano or ELA Soberano) in the Puerto Rican status plebiscite held on November 6, 2012. In the aforementioned process, the ELA Soberano was defined as a free association in accordance with Resolution 1541(XV) of the United Nations, and within the legal framework of the concept as treated in the 2011 Presidential Task Force Report on Puerto Rico's Status.

The CENR has opened verbal participation in the Status Hearing only to the political parties that represented an alternative within the plebiscite. Hence, not being a party, ALAS was not invited. This exclusion was unwarranted. In the plebiscite, the free association alternative obtained 454,768 votes (33.34%). ALAS has therefore been entrusted by these voters with the legal, political and moral right to continue representing them in all matters related to the final status of our country, particularly as it pertains to free association. None of the parties invited to the Status Hearing can legitimately claim this representation.

CENR's actions with respect to ALAS might be construed as an unintentional oversight, but many view it as disrespectful—or at the least, inconsiderate—towards the only organization that has official recognition as the defender of Free Association, an option that may very well become the status preference of the majority of Puerto Rican's, and probably of considerable political convenience for the United States of America as well. I stress this point because future congressional actions may require the representation of the free association option and, at present, that representation falls upon ALAS. This fact should not be overlooked by the CENR if its procedures are truly to be dressed in the cloth of democracy.

THE STATUS PROBLEM

Puerto Rico has been a non-incorporated territory of the United States of America since 1898. As such, it is subject to the absolute powers of Congress over USA territories and possessions. In fact, although Puerto Ricans have been American citizens since 1917, while residing in PR they cannot vote for the President nor can they elect voting representatives to Congress.

In 1952 the Island gained a certain degree of self-government with the creation of the Commonwealth of Puerto Rico, but its colonial nature —or territorial character, if this language suits better—went unchanged. Since its creation, the Commonwealth of Puerto Rico has not evolved towards greater autonomy. On the contrary, federal laws and policies have encroached upon all walks-of-life on the Island, leaving local government with even less authority to manage its own affairs. It is true that during the 50s and 60s the Commonwealth was able to attract outside investment capital, mostly from USA manufacturing companies, to stimulate growth and modernize the Island. However, since the late 1970s PR has actually stopped growing in real terms.

Most Puerto Rican economists equate PR's economic transition —from an agriculture-based society to an industrial-based society—to the stimuli provided by the extraordinary USA economic expansion during the postwar years. A higher educational level achieved during the same period added to that development. But conditions have changed. The world moved towards greater international cooperation and free commerce. As the USA opened its commercial borders to other countries, PR lost one of its principal competitive advantages: unique access to the USA market. Also, PR's fiscal autonomy was impaired since its powers to impose commercial tariffs to imported goods —to protect agriculture and other emerging economic activities—was infringed by several free-trade agreements negotiated by the USA, not necessarily taking PR's best interest into account. In addition, Section 936 of the USA Tax Code was repealed in order to terminate federal tax exemptions to American companies established in PR. Gradually, the islands' industrial base diminished. The default, however, was not compensated by new economic activities but rather by an unhealthy increase in federal transfers. From PR's perspective little else could be done, since the development of a self-sustaining economy required the exercise of sovereign powers, not at its disposal.

We will not enter into the details of the social and economic crisis of Puerto Rico since it is well documented in other writings, and certainly known to the members of the Senate Committee on Energy and Natural Resources. Suffice it to say that it is linked to the political status of PR, thus making the solution of the status problem a critical necessity.

The relation between the deteriorated conditions of PR and its territorial status is not a simple allegation of ALAS. In fact, it has been plainly acknowledged by the White House Task Force on Puerto Rico's Political Status. In its 2005 report to President Obama, the Task Force clearly states that ". . . the status question and the economy are intimately linked. . . And although there are a number of economic actions that should be taken immediately or in the short term, regardless of the ultimate outcome of the status question, identifying the most effective means of assisting the Puerto Rican economy depends on resolving the ultimate question of status."

PUERTO RICO'S POLITICAL RESPONSE

Most Puerto Rican professionals and the middle working class object to the policy of dependency—fostered by all USA Administrations—whereby PR's poor receive social aid through many federal programs, but the Island's economic system is left to fend on its own. As a result, dependency grows and development stalls. Some see this situation as stemming from a lack of adequate federal attention on Puerto Rican affairs. Others see it as a result of federally imposed dispositions approved without regard to PR's needs and economic realities, crippling its capabilities for self-sustained development. As a result, two conflicting paradigms have emerged. One looks upon continued U.S. federal intervention as a solution, the other seeks self-sufficiency through the exercise of sovereign powers.

The group in favor of more USA intervention may be divided into status quo defenders and advocates for federal statehood. The former argue that with assured federal aid and adequate economic policies hard times will eventually subside. The latter speak of acquiring political equality with fellow Americans, through Statehood, while sharing the responsibilities of American citizenship. But their emphasis is on financial matters, disregarding cultural and political complexities. They sustain that the immediate effect of Statehood is a leap in federal funds and that over 80% of Puerto Ricans will not have to pay federal taxes because of their limited incomes. Therefore, Statehood is actually favored on the basis of extending the already ignominious system of dependency.

Another group, which includes ALAS, departs from that view. They argue that PR's economic strategies must arise from its particular realities (language and cultural affinity to Latin America, geographic location, technological capabilities, per capita income, etc.), which are not all similar to those of the USA. Within federal statehood PR would be forced to operate in direct competition with other states from a disadvantaged starting point. The best option is to transform PR into a sovereign state. And, from ALAS's perspective, since the vast majority of Puerto Ricans wish to conserve their American citizenship and collaborative ties with the USA, the best move is not towards traditional independence but towards a sovereign freely associated state.

THE NOVEMBER 2012 PLEBISCITE

In search of a resolution for our status question, several plebiscites have been held; the latest on November 6, 2012. That plebiscite posed two questions related to the political status problem. The first required the voters to state whether or not they were satisfied with the present territorial condition. The second asked them to state their preference for Statehood, Independence or a Sovereign Free Associated State, regardless of how they voted on the first question.

Appendix 1 and Appendix 2* summarize the results for Question 1 and Question 2, respectively. Two perspectives are presented for Question 2. One includes only correctly marked ballots. The other accounts for blank votes, since, as we explain below, they are actually protest votes and should not be ignored.

The voting list contained 1,879,202 voters, a turnout of 78% of all qualified voters and a uniquely high percentage for a plebiscite or referendum in Puerto Rico. On the first question, 54% of the valid votes said NO. In fact, one may assume that many more would have voted NO had it not been because the Popular Democratic Party (PPD) —the party that actually won the general elections held on the same day of the plebiscite—was against the plebiscite and asked the voters to vote YES, as a form of protest. The PPD also asked its followers to leave the second question unanswered. Its aim was to cancel the validity of the vote on that question, since their favored alternative, Enhanced Commonwealth, was not included as an explicit option[1]. Some pro independence groups were also in favor of boycotting the plebiscite.

Excluding null and blank votes, Statehood obtained 61% of the vote; Sovereign Free Association, 33%; and Independence 6%. It would seem that Statehood was the clear victor. But following the PPD's suggestion, 26% of total participants left the second question blank. There is overall agreement that these voters are not in favor of Statehood, but rather inclined towards Independence, Sovereign Free Association or some kind of enhanced Commonwealth. Therefore, when the blank votes are factored in as protest votes, the absolute majority (55%) is actually against Statehood.

Contrary to the protest votes in the second question, only 4% of plebiscite voters abstained from answering the first, so the plea for not continuing as a territory, that is, the call for decolonization of PR is valid and must be addressed by the USA. But, which is the preferred alternative? As we have seen, that question has not yet been answered in a clear-cut fashion, certainly not by an absolute majority of the voters. But it ought to be. And the USA has a political and moral obligation to pave the way so the people of PR can decide.

THE RESPONSIBILITY OF THE UNITED STATES OF AMERICA

Until very recently the USA could cope with the political status problem of PR by arguing that the majority of Puerto Ricans actually favored the status quo; that is, the Commonwealth status. Not anymore. The November 2012 plebiscite shows that an absolute majority is not satisfied with continuing under a territorial status. The argument is proven wrong.

At this moment both Statehood and Sovereign Free Association have a noticeable group behind them. But both paradigms are dependent on the willingness of the USA towards their fulfillment. It is time for Congress to step in and speak truthfully and clearly to the people of PR as to what the USA is willing to concede. Honesty will pave the way to a quick and decisive decision on the part of PR.

One can argue that from the standpoint of the USA, statehood for PR has two overwhelming problems to overcome. First, there is the cultural situation. Puerto Rico is a Latin American nation in its own right and Spanish is its mother language. Can the USA integrate such a nation into itself without risking its own national cohesion and identity or will it insist on PR's cultural assimilation as a precondition to Statehood? The other problem is economical. Will the USA Congress require PR to achieve an economy comparable at least to the poorest USA state so

---

*Appendix 1–2 have been retained in committee files.

[1] The PPD considered the wording of the first question to be unfairly biased against Commonwealth, to favor Statehood. Also, it claimed that the plebiscite was a strategy of the governing New Progressive Party to confuse the political issues in play during the general elections. To counter this, PPD leaders asked voters to oppose the strategy by voting "Yes" to Question 1 and abstaining from voting on Question 2.

that PR can share the tax burdens of Statehood, or will it grant federal statehood regardless of actual economic conditions? If the latter, how will Congress convince the other states that this will not be unfair to them? Clearly it would be better for the USA if it did not have to face these excruciating questions. To do so, the USA would have to steer public opinion in PR towards an alternative other than Statehood.

At present, strictly based on electoral results, Independence cannot pose as a solution either. But the recent plebiscite shows the opening of a new door: Sovereign Free Association. The United Nations acknowledges the status of free association as a means for decolonization and so does the USA. In fact, Congress' recognition and validation of the political viability and significance of this status is exemplified by its approval of three Compacts of Free Associations between the USA and several Pacific island/nations[2]. This is a fortunate situation for both PR and the USA since it opens an avenue for decolonization that avoids the cultural and economic inconveniences of statehood for PR and, for most Puerto Ricans, the unfounded notion of full Independence as an unacceptable risk. A clear message from the USA stating that it is willing to support a compact of free association with PR, upholding American citizenship, would pave the way.

The USA is expected to act, not only from a domestic perspective but an international one as well. When in 1953 the United Nations took note of the creation of the Commonwealth of Puerto Rico and considered it to be an adequate measure of self-government, it expressed its understanding that the newly created political entity was an association open to change. Specifically, in item 9 of UN Resolution 748 (VIII)—1953, the following is stated:

> [The United Nations] expresses its assurance that, in accordance with the spirit of the present resolution . . ., due regard will be paid to the will of both the Puerto Rican and American peoples in the conduct of their relation under the present political statute, and also in the eventuality that either of the parties to the mutually agreed association may desire any change in the terms of this association. (Emphasis added.)

The USA favored the resolution in all its parts. In fact, Henry Cabot Lodge II, at the time USA ambassador to the UN, openly said that the USA would respond positively to any petition of Puerto Rico to modify its political status in the future. Therefore, one can argue that, among others, the cited resolution gives rise to a legal obligation under International Law whereby the USA is required to respond to the will of the Puerto Rican people, in terms of facilitating their self-determination.

Has the USA responded to its obligation to the people of Puerto Rico? Has it taken appropriate steps to facilitate a fair and legitimate act of self-determination so PR can overcome its colonial or territorial limitations? Clearly it has not. But it can, and it should.

PROCEDURAL ALTERNATIVES

Two White House task forces especially convened to study the political status problem of Puerto Rico, one under President George Bush[3]—reports submitted in 2005 and 2007—and the other under President Barack Obama—report submitted in 2011. Both task forces concluded that the present Commonwealth is a non-incorporated territory, still under congressional authority, by virtue of the Territory Clause of the United States of America Constitution. This is the root-cause of the status problem. Therefore, only alternatives that have the effect of taking Puerto Rico out of the Territory Clause are appropriate. For this purpose, two major mechanisms have been recognized as having the highest probability of success in the case of PR: (1) A legally binding plebiscite with definitions approved by federal statute followed by self-executing administrative and legal actions to implement the winning alternative; (2) A Status Constitutional Assembly elected in PR with legal powers to negotiate a status solution with the federal government.

Locally sponsored plebiscites to gage peoples' preferences have their usefulness, but they also have critical limitations. When properly and fairly designed they can point in the direction of preference of the general population. This knowledge can help both countries, Puerto Rico and the United States of America, to gear or direct public efforts in a direction that is most likely to produce fast results that are of

---

[2] These Pacific islands were Strategic Trusteeships administered by the USA under the United Nations supervision. The trusteeships were superseded by these Free Association compacts.

[3] The President's Task Force on Puerto Rico's Status was initially created by President Clinton in 2000.

general acceptance. For example, although the November 2012 plebiscite is non-binding and, some argue, not very well designed, it produced an undeniable and un-ambiguous result for Question 1: The present territorial status embodied in the Commonwealth has been clearly repudiated by an absolute majority of the voters. This result generates a legal, ethical, moral, and political mandate on the USA to quickly address the issue.

But, one must acknowledge that local plebiscites are subject to in-house political play. The greatest drawbacks have been in the arbitrariness of some status definitions or in their representation to the voters. This is particularly true for alternatives that require acquiescence from the USA. Should people vote for statehood if the USA is unwilling to grant it? Or, even if it is willing, should the attributes of statehood be liberally determined by the interested parties in PR? Is it fair to equate a treaty of sovereign free association with a traditional form of independence? Can Puerto Rican politicians be allowed to propose enhancements to the present Commonwealth to a degree that leaves it under the Territory Clause, but denies Congress the exercise of the powers that stem from that clause[4]?

Clearly, in those circumstances, self-determination is not well served. The direct participation of Congress in the definition of these options and being honest and forthright in the alternatives that it is willing to concede, would go a long way to discard false pretensions and coalesce popular opinion into an absolute majority in favor of a non-territorial alternative to Commonwealth. This is why most Puerto Ricans favor a federally designed self-executing status plebiscite. And this is what ALAS also favors.

ALAS recognizes that there are several ways to channel a federally sponsored plebiscite; for example, Bill HR 2000 presented in the House of Representatives by our Resident Commissioner, Hon. Pedro Pierluisi. According to HR 2000, a YES or NO plebiscite for statehood is to be held. If statehood is the victor, Congress is required to design a self-executing mechanism that, over a specified period, would culminate into statehood for Puerto Rico. But if statehood were rejected, no alternative is proposed. In ALAS we favor the statehood YES or NO plebiscite, but add that if the NO carries, another plebiscite should follow, posing independence against sovereign free association. With this mechanism a resolution to the status problem would be definite. In lack of said mechanism, HR 2000 fails the requirements of an acceptable self-determination process.

President Barack Obama seems to be taking an intermediate approach. The Administration would provide $2.5 Million to finance a locally designed plebiscite, but requiring the following: "The monies could be used after the Attorney General has found a Commission plan that includes education materials and ballot options to be consistent with the Constitution and basic laws and policies of the United States of America."

The Obama proposal falls short of what was expected, on two accounts:

- It is financially insufficient. Clearly such an electoral event would require a much higher budgetary assignment, at least double the amount.
- It does not lead to a definite solution to the status problem and it does not preclude including the present Commonwealth as an option. The latter is particularly objectionable, for Commonwealth is the very source of the territorial problem, and besides, it has already been rejected in the very recent plebiscite. Given these shortcomings, although ALAS is still open to the President's proposal, our final stand on the matter would depend on the particulars of the referendum once specifically defined. In a letter to the President, dated April 22, 2012, ALAS expressed its position as follows:

> Thus, we welcome your recommendation. However, as proposed, it falls short as it does not meet the rightful expectation of the people of Puerto Rico to engage in a legally binding and congressionally sponsored plebiscite, with realistic status definitions. Nevertheless, we consider your suggestion as an opportunity to exercise our right to self-determination facing status options that meet federal criteria, at least from the point of view of the Executive Branch, and in accordance to international law and agreements.

> We are convinced that, if definitions of final status options are worked out with legal thoroughness and political honesty and if a rigorous and comprehensive voter education plan is implemented, the proposed plebiscite should provide Puerto Ricans important clarifications and tools to press forward the decolonization process to a relatively rapid resolution.

---

[4] The White House Reports have denied that possibility on constitutional grounds, but PPD leaders allege that it is already so because of Supreme Court decisions. Who are we to believe?

The Status Constitutional Assembly (SCA) is another possibility. But it too has its implementation complexities. For one, it is not a simple matter to determine how it will be constituted; many different proposals have been presented, hinting that it would not be a straightforward matter. Another difficulty is coordination with the USA. Will the USA acknowledge the SCA? Will the SCA negotiate with the Executive Administration or Congress? Of course, these details can be worked out if there is a will to solve the status problem. Again, the USA must be forthright and make its collaboration efforts apparent with no ambiguity of purpose.

CLOSING REMARKS

The alleged popular support for the territorial Commonwealth of Puerto Rico has been pierced by the results of the plebiscite celebrated in November 2012. The stark reality is that Congress exerts its territorial powers over the island against our people's will.

The United States of America —through the President and Congress—has a moral as well as a legal obligation to respond democratically, effectively, and promptly to this situation. Will it do so as a nation true to its beginnings or is it still stuck in the outdated paradigms of colonialism?

The time to act is now.

————

STATEMENT OF HON. LUIS VEGA-RAMOS, MEMBER OF THE PUERTO RICO HOUSE OF REPRESENTATIVES AND CHAIRMAN OF THE HOUSE JUDICIARY COMMITTEE

My name is Luis Vega-Ramos. I am Member of the House of Representatives of Puerto Rico elected on behalf of the Popular Democratic Party (PDP).

I also present this statement on behalf of the following elected officials of the PDP: the Mayor of San Juan, Hon. Carmen Yulin Cruz-Soto, the Mayor of Caguas, Hon. William Miranda-Torres, the Mayor of Comerío, Hon José A. Santiago, the Mayor of Hormigueros, Hon. Pedro García, the Mayor of San Germán, Hon. Isidro Negrón, the Mayor of Isabela, Hon. Charlie Delgado, representatives Luis Raúl Torres, Carlos Vargas-Ferrer, Carlos Bianchi, Luisa "Piti" Gándara-Menéndez and Charlie Hernández-López and the majority leader of the Municipal Assembly of San Juan, Marco A. Rigau.

Last November 6th, along with our general elections, the previous pro-Statehood government held a referendum that posed two questions on the issue of Puerto Rico's political status. Said plebiscite was held with the objections of large segments of our society, including the Popular Democratic Party.

Regrettably, the expression of an overwhelming majority in favor of a process to produce changes to the political status of Puerto Rico was thwarted as a direct consequence of the timing of the vote and of the politically charged language of the first question in the ballot.

With regards to the second question, an important clarification is in order. Puerto Rico's Senate Concurrent Resolution No. 24, recently approved by both Houses of our Legislature, correctly states that: "Supporters of Estado Libre Asociado (Commonwealth) expressed themselves through two protest mechanisms. On one side, the Governing Board of the pro-Commonwealth Party adopted a resolution asking voters to deposit a blank ballot in protest. On the other side, a significant number of pro-Commonwealth leaders openly campaigned in favor of a vote for the option called Estado Libre Asociado Soberano (Sovereign Commonwealth)."

The elected officials that file this testimony are among those that campaigned and voted against Statehood through the option of Estado Libre Asociado Soberano (Sovereign Commonwealth). We present this statement on behalf of the more than 454.000 Puerto Rican voters who also voted that way. It is our duty to expose the misrepresentation of the results of the so-called plebiscite of 2012 by the leaders of the pro-Statehood Party. We also want to reiterate our demand that the U.S. Government enact now, a binding, self-executing mechanism in furtherance of our demands for Puerto Rican self-determination, But in the event that Congress and the Administration fail once more in providing for such a process during the remainder of this year, we inform you that we will advocate for the convening by the Puerto Rican Legislature of a special Constitutional Assembly on Status as the best way to achieve this purpose.

To this end, we state for the record the following:

1. That the economic and social situation of Puerto Rico requires organizing responsibly and diligently the matter of our self-determination to avoid conflict with ongoing recovery efforts, and to substantially accelerate the benefits that the resolution of the issue will bring. There is no contradiction between working

for economic improvements today and simultaneously promoting self-determination.

2. It is misleading to claim that the option of Statehood won last year's plebiscite with a majority of 61% of voters. When you add up the votes of all other participants: Independence (74,894/ 4%), Sovereign Commonwealth (454,768/ 24.3%) and blank ballots (498,604/ 26.5%), the votes cast for Statehood do not surmount its traditional 45% support. The majority of the votes on last November's status plebiscite were cast against the Statehood option.

3. That to secure democratic validity of any process, it is necessary to include all sectors of the debate. That means properly allowing for the discussion and consideration of all options including, among others, the non-territorial aspirations of those who seek to develop the Commonwealth status through. what former Governor Luis Muñoz Marín called in 1962, "the sovereign capacity of the people of Puerto Rico",

4. That the Constitutional Status Assembly is the appropriate mechanism to address the issue of political status. We filed in the Puerto Rico's House of Representatives, Bill No, 210, drafted by the Constitutional Development Commission of the Puerto Rico Bar Association, which provides for the convening and functioning of the Constitutional Assembly on Status. Various members of the Puerto Rico Senate have recently stated that they will file a similar bill during this month. The PDP Platform, also approved by voters last November, states the following: "If after one year, the White House has not fulfilled its pledge, meaning, that the President has not presented a bill before Congress to enact a referendum on which the United States commits to abide by the totality of the decision of the people of Puerto Rico, the Governor will move forward with a Constitutional Assembly to deal with the issue of status. To that end, the Popular Party formally commits to enacting legislation to convene a Constitutional Assembly on Status. Any proposal for a change in status that is recommended as a result of the proceedings of the Constitutional Assembly will have to be presented to voters in a special referendum as an indispensable condition for its approval or rejection."

The fate of President Obama's proposal on status included on the budget presented to Congress will be known by October 1, when the new federal fiscal year begins. In its current form, it falls short of being a bill before Congress that would enact a binding plebiscite. But even if President Obama's proposal is approved, nothing prevents it from being tempered to work within the framework of a Constitutional Assembly on Status convened by Puerto Rico. In that regard, we suggest that you look into S.2304 filed by Senators Burr, Kennedy, Lott and Menendez during the 109th Congress as a starting point.

There is an additional issue of importance. Last May, Oscar Lopez-Rivera reached the unacceptable milestone of serving 32 years in confinement as a Puerto Rican political prisoner in the U.S. correctional system. The call to President Obama advocating for his immediate and unconditional release has overwhelming support among Puerto Ricans of all political ideologies. Recently, both the House of Representatives and the Senate of Puerto Rico passed resolutions reiterating this position to the President of the United States. Governor Alejandro Garcia-Padilla has also requested this action. We bring to your attention that Mr. Oscar Lopez-Rivera's release is an important step towards Puerto Rico's self-determination process.

Thank you very much.

———

STATEMENT OF MANUEL RIVERA, LOBBYIST FOR PUERTO RICO'S SOVEREIGNTY MOVEMENT, INCLUDING BUT NOT LIMITED TO THE FOLLOWING CIVIL SOCIETY NON-POLITICAL PARTIES ORGANIZATIONS: MOVIMIENTO INDEPENDENTISTA NACIONAL HOSTOCIANO (MINH); ACCION DEMOCRATICA PUERTORRIQUENA (ADP); PROELA; MOVIMIENTO SEIS DE MAYO; ALIANZA PRO LIBRE ASOCIACION SOBERANA (ALAS); PUERTORRIQUENOS UNIDOS EN ACCION (PUA)

Mr. Chairman and Members of the Committee.

I appreciate the opportunity to present my statement in writing before the Senate Committee on Energy and Natural Resources on behalf of Puerto Rico's Sovereignty Movement which supports self-determination for Puerto Rico and its diaspora participation.

Much of the public behavior of Puerto Rican politicians in the United States suggests that their electorates are located in Puerto Rico as well as in the United States. Puerto Rico's political status is a primary concern for "transnational" politicians such as Congressman Luis Gutierrez (Illinois), Congressman Jose Serrano

(New York), and Congresswoman Lydia Velazquez (New York), together with other issues that affect U.S. Latinos, such as bilingual education and immigration reform. As recent as the late 1990s and early 2000s, several community leaders from New York, Chicago, and other U.S. cities supported the "Peace for Vieques" movement, which sought to end the U.S. Navy's presence in Vieques, an offshore municipality of Puerto Rico. Among others, the three representatives of Puerto Rican origin were arrested during peaceful manifestations against military operations in Vieques. On May 1, 2003, due to public pressure on the Island and abroad, the US Navy terminated its military exercises in Vieques, following the closing of Roosevelt Road's Naval Base in Ceiba. Similarly, the diaspora has supported the liberation of Puerto Rican political prisoners in U.S. jails. Most recently, the three Puerto Rican representatives in the U.S. Congress and Commissioner Resident of Puerto Rico, Pedro Perluisi, signed a joint letter mailed to President Barack Obama requesting a presidential pardon for Oscar Lopez Rivera, a Puerto Rican national in the diaspora who has attained the status of political prisoner due to his activism for independence.

In various ways, the Puerto Rican diaspora has helped shape U.S. policies toward the Island. However, past administrations have ignored the diaspora's requests to participate in previous plebiscites. Despite endless efforts to amend the legislation that authorized the celebration of the November 6, 2012 plebiscite on the political status of Puerto Rico, the diaspora was barred from participating once again. Thus, a viable solution for diaspora participation can be made by a Constitutional Assembly. On January 2, 2013, Puerto Rico Legislative Representative, Luis Vega Ramos, Chairman of the House of Representative of Puerto Rico's Judiciary Committee, introduced a bill calling for a Constitutional Assembly; a draft legislation prepared by the Comision de Desarrollo Constitucional del Colegio de Abogados de Puerto Rico (Commission for Constitutional Development of the Puerto Rican Bar). This draft legislation for a Constitutional Assembly allows for the participation of our compatriots residing outside the Puerto Rican national territory in the exercise of our self-determination.

Until now, all local elections, referenda, and plebiscites have been restricted to Island residents who meet a residency requirement. Ironically, the plebiscite held in Puerto Rico on November 6, 2012 permitted only those that were able to meet the residency requirements in the country to vote. This procedure that was in effect for the November 6, 2012 plebiscite lacks credibility. Such rules make the plebiscite an arbitrary procedure in that individuals disinterested in the political future of Puerto Rico, such as non-Puerto Rican nationals, were able to participate, and at the same time, the Puerto Rican diaspora was excluded merely on geographical terms. For example, the eligibility criteria established by the law permitted overseas residents living in Puerto Rico for a period of one year to vote in the plebiscite. No one denies that many foreigners have integrated to the extent that many have adopted our nation's customs and mores. Notwithstanding, it is also true, that other foreigners residing on the island temporarily do not feel a connection with our nation.

Puerto Ricans in the United States have reiterated their desire to participate in the definition of the political future of our country. This trend has attained popular support in Puerto Rico. Judging from the available evidence, the ideological preferences of stateside Puerto Ricans are similar to those of Island residents. For example, a public poll sponsored by the newspaper El Nuevo Dia (2004) found that 48 percent of Puerto Ricans in central Florida favored the current Commonwealth status, while 42 percent preferred the Island's annexation as a state of the union and 5 percent supported independence.

In the 1990s, a group of Puerto Rican leaders in New York, including state Senator Jose Rivera, sponsored the first symbolic election. The results showed that Independence attained 30% while Estado Libre Asociado (Commonwealth) obtained 36% and Statehood, 34%.

As a result of circular migration for more than a century, thousands of Puerto Ricans have developed multiple "home bases" in the United States as well as in Puerto Rico, allowing them to keep strong ties with the Island, even while living abroad for long periods. Many people now move routinely between various households, located on the Island and in the diaspora, to expand their survival strategies and strengthen their kinship networks. This phenomenon requires the rethinking of Puerto Rican migration as the spatial extension of family ties through an incessant traffic of persons in both directions. A dense network of transnational connections means that most Puerto Ricans experience migration directly, whether personally or through a close relative. Thus, it is increasingly difficult to draw a sharp line between the Island and its diaspora, given that a substantial proportion of Puerto Ricans spend part of their lives at both poles of the migratory circuit.

The experience of the diaspora suggests that national identities may survive and even prosper for long periods in a foreign country. Since the late nineteenth century, several generations of Puerto Rican migrants have maintained tight links with their country of origin. Their community organizations have selectively appropriated discourses and practices traditionally associated with Puerto Rican culture. The diaspora communities remain tied to the Island through the constant circulation of people, money, material and symbolic goods, and cultural traditions.

The Puerto Rican diaspora has often nurtured "long distance nationalism" by reclaiming an identity rooted in the Island, but increasingly disseminated throughout the U.S. mainland. Nowadays, being born in Puerto Rico, speaking Spanish, and living on the Island are not exclusive markers of Puerto Rican identity.

In sum, the diaspora has broadened the territorial and linguistic borders of the nation. Puerto Rico has become a transnational nation, a country crisscrossed by nomadic subjects moving back and forth between the Island, the U.S. mainland, and other Caribbean countries, especially the Dominican Republic. The crucial challenge posed by the dispersal of the Puerto Rican population is imagining a nation whose physical and symbolic borders are constantly transgressed and redrawn by migration.

REQUIREMENT FOR PUERTO RICANS TO QUALIFY AS VOTERS OVERSEAS

The present electoral laws and procedures in Puerto Rico are antiquated. For example, there are no procedures in place for electronic voting and the votes are tallied by hand. This procedure exposes the process to major electoral fraud. According to Professor of Law Julio Fontanet, and former Electoral Commissioner at the Puerto Rico Electoral Commission for the Movimiento Union Soberanista Party, the recent changes in the electoral laws approved by the previous administration left the current barriers in effect, impeding the diaspora's participation in any future self-determination process.

There are restrictions imposed on Puerto Ricans living outside the national territory which affect their ability to participate in a self-determination process. The ability to vote in Puerto Rico is conditioned on the type of activity that is performed overseas (only citizens included in predefined categories may qualify). For example, voting access is expressly reserved for those who perform official functions (like active members of the Armed Forces of the United States or the National Guard of Puerto Rico, or notable figures in diplomatic service) or perform a certain type of activity outside of the country (like agricultural employees executing a contract negotiated by the Labor Department or foreign exchange students studying at an accredited institution). That is to say, the suffrage guarantee does not include all citizens overseas, as there are express limitations associated with the type of activity that Puerto Ricans can perform overseas.

From a comparative international perspective, an increasing number of other countries in Latin America and Europe permit its diaspora to participate in important electoral contests. However, no other applicable legislation in the Latin America region conditions its nationals' ability to vote on the time spent outside of the country. Therefore, so long as a person can maintain their citizenship he or she retains the ability to vote irrespective of the period that individual has resided outside of the country. This is significant because the Supreme Court of Puerto Rico determined in the case of Miriam Ramirez de Ferrer v. Juan Mari Bras that a citizen of Puerto Rico retains the right to vote irrespective of whether the person renounced his/her U.S. citizenship.

In order to vote in Puerto Rico it is necessary for qualified citizens to have registered previously in the country. In other countries, however, it is sufficient that the citizens execute specific registry documents or register as voters overseas in order to vote outside of their national territory. Further, in other countries there are procedures that permit the voter registration process at sites specifically authorized to perform this function overseas. In principle, the possibility of realizing the registration process overseas represents a convenience for the potential overseas voter as he/she would not be required to return to the country to register to vote.

For example, in the case of the electoral authority in the Dominican Republic, they determined that the voter registry shall only occur in certain cities in five countries (Canada, Spain, United States, Puerto Rico, and Venezuela), where the major concentration of potential voters reside. Honduras, for example, has opted for a very limited scope and concentrated on six cities in the United States: Houston, Los Angeles, Miami, New Orleans, New York, and Washington, D.C.

Although the deadlines usually average a few months, it is worth noting the Dominican Republic for its ample concessions to its voters in the city of New York, who for the first time exercised the vote overseas in the May 2004 elections. The voter registration process was maintained open in that jurisdiction for more than two years, from October 2001 until January 2004.

Puerto Rico breaks from the voter registration process mold of other countries, in that there are no sites outside the national territory authorized to complete the required registry. In Puerto Rico, as previously mentioned, only certain categories of citizens may vote. They also must previously register as voters within the country, because the process that they are able to perform overseas only includes a request to receive and cast a vote by mail—not to register as a voter. This request must be submitted directly to a specific electoral administrative body in Puerto Rico who can designate it as an "absentee vote," (this also includes a method of early voting for certain voters within the national territory) two months in advance of the electoral contest. Moreover, any request for absentee voting from overseas must be accompanied by a certification from a competent authority (a representative of the institution for whom he/she works), who can affirm the conditions of voter eligibility.

Puerto Rico is different from other countries in Latin America or Europe in the way it effectuates overseas suffrage. The usual method requires that the eligible voter appear at places specifically authorized to effectuate the vote. Traditionally, these places are located at the diplomatic or consular headquarters and, when these prove to be inadequate or insufficient due to the number of registered voters, it is done at other sites that offer better security conditions and easily accessible facilities for the casting and counting of ballots. In these cases, it is not uncommon for the leasing of schools or sports facilities or the anticipated use of certain sites utilized by other State-sanctioned functions including commercial centers or national companies, as Brazilian law allows. Only in the case of Dominican Republic, for political reasons, it was decided that for the first presidential election overseas in 2004 it would not assign all diplomatic and consular offices as designated overseas voting precincts.

For an overseas voter to participate in Puerto Rico's elections the casting of votes overseas is done through paper ballots that are received by the voter and must be returned by mail. In order for votes by mail to be valid, it is imperative that the voter appear before some competent authority overseas (military, diplomatic, or consular authority), so that it can certify that the ballot was validly cast in secret and personally cast by the authorized voter. The problem with the electoral process in Puerto Rico is that the access to voting for citizens overseas is expressly reserved, as previously mentioned, for those employed in official State functions.

In order to implement in Puerto Rico a truly democratic self-determination process, the Puerto Rican diaspora must be allowed to participate. A Constitutional Assembly is the way for the people of Puerto Rico to achieve self-determination and preserve the principle of democracy.

I would be happy to respond in writing to any question you might have.

————

Dear Senator Wyden and Committee Members:

For the last 50 years I've been involved in a quest for equality and full democratic participation in our nation's democratic processes for 3.7 million Hispanic Americans in Puerto Rico.

I read the CRS report on Puerto Rico's political status. As a Puerto Rican, as a Hispanic American from Puerto Rico and as an American citizen, I feel outraged at the fact that the CRS report completely sidesteps the issue of discrimination against Hispanic Americans in Puerto Rico. The report completely fails to even mention the inequality, the disfranchisement and the denial of full democracy to Hispanic Americans in Puerto Rico.

Discussion of status is a way to ignore and to keep ignoring the real issue: denial of voting rights, denial of participating in our nation's democratic process and denial of economic equality and opportunities for Hispanic Americans in Puerto Rico.

Our nation is the example and inspiration of democracy throughout the world. It was the inspiration on the Chinese demonstrations in Tiananmen Square; it was the inspiration in the struggle for democracy in the revolution against communist dictatorships in Poland, East Germany, the Soviet Union itself and other nations throughout the world. However, when it comes to existing prejudice and disenfranchisement of 3.7 million Puerto Ricans in our nation's process, everyone looks the other way and talks about status instead of equality and democracy.

As American citizen's we in Puerto Rico are entitled to equal rights, privileges and benefits as well as equal duties and obligations as all other American citizens and as American citizens we are entitled to the right to vote for our President and to full representation in Congress.

The Puerto Rican issue is not status. Our real issue is one of equality and democracy, and until our nation's Congress and our President accept the reality of the discrimination against Hispanic Americans in Puerto Rico which has denied us the right to vote and to participate in our nation's democratic process during the past 96 years, our nation lacks the moral authority to preach democracy throughout the world. How can Congress and the President justify spending billions of dollars and risking the lives of our young men and woman by sending them in harm's way to take "democracy" to Irak and Afganistan, who do not want nor do they fully understand democracy, while denying equality and participation in our Nation's democratic processes to 3.7 million Hispanic Americans in Puerto Rico, who are natural born American citizens?

Our nation's Congress has the duty to recognize this discrimination as it has recognized the discrimination against African Americans, against the LGBT groups, and we are presently discussing discrimination against Hispanic American immigrants who are not citizens.

Until the discrimination against the Hispanic Americans in Puerto Rico is acknowledged, our nation has no moral authority to preach democracy around the world. It is important that the issue of equality and democracy for Puerto Rican Americans be addressed NOW.

Yours truly,

CARLOS ROMERO BARCELÓ,
Governor of Puerto Rico,
(1977-1985).

○